I believe that in South Africa as in any other place in the world, an honest discussion about sexual assault, women's oppression and women's safety needs to begin with how we raise men. I'd like to move beyond the developed world's approach to teaching women to empower themselves because – as I once announced to a room full of appalled first-world feminists – telling women to end rape is like telling black people to end racism. It seems counter-productive to me. When your child comes home from school after being bullied it's best to address the bully's behaviour instead of wondering what your child can do to stop it. There are basic behaviour patterns that need to be completely altered. Much of what we need to do, I think, lies in what boys learn – from both men and women – as they grow up.

– Kagiso Lesego Molope, novelist

Physical pain aside, the enduring trauma of rape is that, like slavery, it makes of a person a thing. It denies human subjectivity. Despite every effort, it is impossible not to replay the memory of this over and over again in one's mind. In the absence of therapeutic alternatives, the only way to resolve this vicious cycle and restore her status as a subject is to de-objectify the rapist to argue 'it was all a mistake' or even 'I didn't really mind'. Thus denial on the part of a rape victim can occur as a result of both the rape and the repeated trauma of remembering her rape.

– Yvette Abrahams,
Women and Gender Studies Department, UWC

To what extent is it even possible to resist and transform the social languages into which we are born? More to the point, how does one challenge the gendered norms that lead to the formatio̶ *patriarchal and violent m*

– Helene Strauss, University

First published by MFBooks Joburg, an imprint of
Jacana Media (Pty) Ltd, in 2015

10 Orange Street
Sunnyside
Auckland Park 2092
South Africa
+2711 628 3200
www.jacana.co.za

ISBN 978-1-920601-52-2

Cover design by Shawn Paikin
Set in Sabon 11/15pt
Printed and bound by ABC Press, Cape Town
Job no. 002560

Also available as an e-book:
d-PDF: 978-1-920601-53-9
ePUB: 978-1-920601-54-6
mobi file: 978-1-920601-55-3

See a complete list of Jacana titles at www.jacana.co.za

Rape

A South African nightmare

Pumla Dineo Gqola

Contents

Acknowledgements.. vii
Introduction 1

Chapter 1: A recurring nightmare 21
Chapter 2: What's race got to do with rape?.................. 37
Chapter 3: Ruling violence..................................... 54
Chapter 4: The female fear factory 78
Chapter 5: Making sense of responses to the Jacob Zuma
        rape trial.. 100
Chapter 6: Forked tongue on child rape 125
Chapter 7: Rape myths.. 143
Chapter 8: Violent masculinities and war talk............... 152

Conclusion 168
Bibliography.. 180

Acknowledgements

The insights in this book are drawn from what I have been taught by observing and reading the work of numerous people, as well as from conversations over a lifetime, even though the limitations are all mine. I am grateful to Nombulelo Ncata, Bulela Mjika, Vuyolwethu Mabeqa for things too numerous to mention, but especially the capacity to choose the more difficult option, to confront the truth when this was not easy, and the capacity for love, as well as for loyalty, to principle and other girls, long before any of us had ever heard the words 'feminism' or 'women's empowerment' or 'queer'. I am also grateful to them for the many things that they probably did not even realise they were teaching me. Noluthando Qongqo, the late Nomfanelo Nongongo and Lulama Nongogo, thank you for a conversation that changed my outlook on rape and for having my back. Thumeka Scwebu, Unathi Conjwa, Thozama Vokwana, Thulani Khanyile, Angelo Fick and Madi Jenneker thank you inspiring me with courage, and for being everything. Penny Parenzee, Ayanda Mvimbi, Ingrid Masondo, Vuyo Koyana, Nomfundo Walaza for Rape Crisis lessons too many to mention and teaching me how to concretely contribute to the fight against patriarchal violence. Caroline Skinner, Thandi Lewin, Paula Kingwill, Ruth Hall, Wendy Woodward and Thandeka Kunene, thank you for being my community of undergrad feminist troublemakers at Gender SubCom, Women's Forum and Women's Movement, UCT, but decidedly not for all the time we spent bromiding posters. Shireen Hassim and Jacklyn Cock, thank you for pushing me to go further in my thinking and for reflections on the language with which to say it; this book and the next would not have been written without you. Desiree Lewis, Mary Hames, Elaine Salo, Jane Bennett, Helene Strauss, I am grateful for inspirational work that always stretches and inspires me, even when we have disagreed. Wendy Isaack, Bunie Matlanyane Sexwale, Prudence Mabele, Mmatshilo Motsei, Nokuthula Mazibuko Msimang, Steve Letsike, Carrie Shelver, Kwezilomso Mbandazayo, Mpumi Mathabela, Mpumi Simelane, Thamsanqa Scaps Zulu, Neo Sinoxolo Musangi, Prudence Mabele, Pumeza Ceza, Xoliswa Sithole, Kodwa Tyiso, Donna Smith, Zanele Muholi and Den Ngoqo, I am in awe of your brains and courage. Thank you to everybody at One in Nine. Simmi Dullay, Lungisa Mkentane, thank you for your open hearts and generosity at times when courage would be impossible for most. Thank you to the many women, whose names I cannot mention, who have trusted me, taught me and held me accountable.

Chapter 3 has a previous life as the Ruth First lecture "After Zuma: rape and the Constitution" presented at Constitution Hill on 15 November 2006. Extracts from this lecture were published as 'The hype of women's empowerment' in *Mail and Guardian*, 23–30 November 2006, as well as "Gender talk is seriously flawed" in *Cape Times*, 27 November 2006. The revised lecture appeared in academic form as "How the 'cult of femininity' and violent masculinities support endemic gender based violence in contemporary South Africa", published in *African Identities* 5.1(2007):111-124. I am grateful to the Ruth First Fellowship Committee, and especially Shireen Hassim and Jacklyn Cock, who read and commented on drafts, and the Heinrich Böll Stiftung for the time to write and rewrite. Chapter 8 draws extensively from, revises and expands arguments first made in "'The difficult task of normalising freedom': spectacular masculinities, Ndebele's literary/cultural commentary and post-apartheid life", published in *English in Africa* 36.1(2009): 61-76. Different parts of the book contain arguments from "2013 is a bad year for gender struggle: GBV, South Africa and feministing differently", presented at the African Gender Institute Talking the Walk Lecture on 29 April 2013 at All Africa House, University of Cape Town. The event was co-hosted by the Centre for Women and Gender Studies and Gender Equity Unit, both at the University of the Western Cape. I am grateful to Jane Bennett, Desiree Lewis and Mary Hames, for the resources and time they allocated me to write, present and reflect on the presentation, as well as for the conversation and community they made possible. Some arguments in this paper were also previously explored in "If sexuality is the new religion, how do we avoid fundamentalism?", a public lecture presented at the University of the Western Cape on 24 April 2007 on the invitation of former Minister Z Pallo Jordan during his tenure at the Department of Arts and Culture. I am indebted to all the questions, comments, provocations and conversations that happened after these lectures and seminars at the University of the Western Cape, University of Fort Hare, University of Cape Town, University of the Free State and various places in the Eastern Cape and Johannesburg. None of the chapters or lectures appear here verbatim from any of the previous sources of presentation or publication.

Grace Musila, thank you, again, for meticulous reading, incisive feedback and elegant editing of another manuscript from me. Melinda Ferguson, whose patience I test way beyond the reasonable, thank you for being a dream publisher once again, and for saying "We're not robots, we're human beings". Danai Mupotsa, I just cannot believe your mind. You are such a treasure.

To my friends, Dina Ligaga and Sarah Chiumbu, whose minds and presence are an enormous gift to me, who go to lunch with me when I have writer's block or am too afraid to write, and help me put it all in perspective. I don't know what I ever did without you. Thank you.

Finally, thank you to my family: my mother, my siblings, son, partner and bestie for your patience in dealing with my emotional unavailability as I took much longer to write this book than I said I would, my falling asleep mid-conversation, cancelled plans, crankiness, unreturned phone calls, sleeping all day and working all night, late collections and everything else that complicated our lives.

Introduction

Many years ago, I watched a television programme where a journalist and cameraperson sat around and talked to a group of young men who readily admitted on camera to having raped. It was a strange and unsettling encounter. It was also illuminating. The journalist was a woman and her questions probed the motivations, the styles and the patterns of the young men she interviewed. Something made them feel safe enough to talk to her on camera, but I can no longer remember whether their faces were obscured or whether they had been convicted and served jail sentences for rape. Whatever it was, it allowed a level of candour that is often absent from South African public talk on rape.

I can only remember one other similar conversation aired a few years later with young men who had raped Black lesbians specifically. It was a programme primarily devoted to survivors of rape, but at the end airplay was given to men who targeted out Black lesbians, gender non-confirming people, and women they suspected of being lesbian.

Because there is so much talk of rape and 'corrective'/'curative' rape in South African media, I have not been able to find the footage I am recalling. I only remember how long ago and how far apart the screenings were because of where I lived when I watched them. But perhaps that allows me to work with why these two programmes made such an impression on me that they retain a grip on my imagination so many years later. In both, the rapists were unrepentant and laughing uncomfortably; and in the first programme they were sharing anecdotes. The interviewers grew visibly more flustered at the absence of remorse. Some of the men reported that they were no longer serial rapists, but most admitted that they would probably rape again.

In these instances, those who had retired from raping had done so due to something that had nothing to do with rape. They had generally stopped committing crime of various sorts, or had stopped the drug-taking that they partly attributed the rapes to, or some other lifestyle shift. The ones who did not speak of rape as something they did in the past admitted that they saw nothing wrong with raping. All of them insisted that it was a type of sex that they were entitled to. None of them wanted to admit that it was violence that had far-reaching effects, that they could ruin women's lives, and that rape traumatises. They all insisted that while it was obviously unpleasant to be forced to do anything, the effects of rape were not long-term wounding. They also reported not suffering any real consequences themselves from a life of serially raping women. By real consequences, I refer to the fact that there had been no social cost to raping women directly. None of their relationships had suffered. They had not been ostracised or stigmatised. Even when coming out of jail for rape convictions, the argument that they had served their time and therefore required a second chance mediated societal responses to them, even if prior convictions and imprisonment does not always curtail subsequent decisions to rape.

Then something interesting happened in the first interview. The journalist asked how they would feel if a woman they loved was raped: a sister or a niece, specifically, rather than a mother or a partner. All of them were disturbed by this question, with one man swearing he would kill a man who dared hurt his sister.

The interviewer's point had been made: one about the connections between his hypocrisy and brutality. If they genuinely did not find their behaviour harmful, then the consistency with which they wanted to keep the women and girls they loved safe from rape did not make sense. Clearly, these men were not ignorant of the effects of their actions. They raped because they *could*, and in this decision was the implicit statement that some women did not matter. Therefore, violating them is permissible.

The second programme was stranger still because the conversation with the rapists sat so oddly at the end of what had been a very sympathetic and sensitive series of conversations with young lesbians who had either been raped themselves or supported loved ones who had been raped. These men spoke unequivocally of their entitlement to teach these women a lesson that men would have access to their bodies regardless of what they wanted. Rape, here, was explicitly a weapon. There was no doublespeak, no excuses.

I am working from memory, and memory is unreliable, so there are aspects of the programmes that I may have edited out. I start with this recollection because these shows offered rare public access to the mind of a rapist. In most public talk, people distance themselves from rape and express incomprehension about how rape continues to have such a firm grip on our society. These men were not animals or monsters. They looked like anybody's brother, boyfriend or son. There is no way to tell who can choose to rape, even though women and girls are often told that they can protect themselves by staying away from certain places and kinds of men. Rapists can be anywhere and everywhere; rape culture and the manufacture of female fear (which I also call the female fear factory) are part of how we collectively get socialised to accept the ever-presence of rape most often by being invited to be vigilant. The female fear factory is a subject I dedicate Chapter 4 to.

To start with this anecdote does not mean that these men verbalised something we might want to think of as 'typical' of rapist behaviour. This clearly is not the case. We do not have brazen admissions of having raped women by all the men who have in fact done so. Rather, what is important about these two programmes is the notion that women's pain is negotiable, that while rapists know (because how can they not) that they inflict harm, they proceed to do so in any event. And they do so often, knowing that many will

3

line up alongside them to defend them against such accusation, requiring evidence and the legal reporting. They also know of the high likelihood that they will be acquitted in legal courts and the court of public opinion.

It is a myth that rapists come from a certain background, race, class location or religion. At the same time, there are very specific reasons why so many people continue to believe that some groups of men are more likely to be rapists than others. In the long 2004 public argument with Charlene Smith, former South African president Thabo Mbeki was not entirely off the mark when he insisted that we need to interrogate the automatic links made between Black men and rape. At the same time, Charlene Smith was correct to point out the prevalence of rape and its unacceptability. The stereotype of the Black male rapist of white women has been central to the rise of racism, and it has also been used as justification for lynching and killing tens of thousands of Black men across the globe – in the Americas, on the African continent and in South Asia. I am using capitalised Black here to refer to black and brown people, in other words, the collective people of African and South Asian descent. This is not a small matter, and constructions of 'black peril', or what was termed *'swaartgevaar'* in colonial and apartheid South Africa, depended heavily on this idea of the sexually and otherwise violent Black man. So, we do need to constantly guard against reliance on stereotype to explain rape and to fight for its end. At the same time, guarding against stereotype cannot be justification to silence activism against rape. To say a stereotype exists does not mean that Black men never rape women of any race. Most rape survivors in South Africa are Black because most people in South Africa are Black; that seems quite straightforward. However, there is a much more insidious reason for the large numbers of rape than numbers. The same white supremacy that constructed the stereotype of Black man as rapist, created the stereotype of Black women as hypersexual and therefore impossible to rape. Making Black women *impossible* to rape does not mean making them *safe* against rape. It means quite the opposite: that Black women are safe to rape, that raping them does not count as harm and is therefore permissible. It also means that it is not an accident that when Black women say they have been raped, they are almost never taken seriously and in many instances are expected to just get over it.

In Chapter 2, I briefly trace how this came to be so. I do not expect you to just take my word for it, and, if this chapter piques your curiosity, there is a wealth of scholarship that demonstrates how this is true in relation to East African, American and South Asian contexts too. It is not an accident that the explosions and brazen instances of rape in South Africa and India have been so remarkably similar in recent years. Part of this history of who becomes safe to rape, and safe to construct as unrapable is directly linked to this history. Here, and throughout this book, I use unrapable and impossible to rape to mean the same thing: the creation of the racist myth that this is so also makes it possible for those coded as unrapable to be habitually raped as a matter of course.

In Chapter 2, I also trace the long history of rape in South Africa, unpack the pornography of empire, and demonstrate how it is that although all women are in danger of rape, Black women are the most likely to be raped. It is not for the reasons that would seem 'logical' or obvious. It has little to do with numbers, and much to do with how rape and race have historically intersected in mutually reinforcing ways. In this chapter, I show that these examples are different racist regimes.

Chapter 1 is linked to this project because it is also about thinking through the contexts that help us make sense of rape. In this first chapter I am also interested in why so many in our society are able to believe *some* rape survivors so easily and refuse to believe others. Some of this has to do with the myth that 'real' rape looks a certain way or that all survivors behave in the same kinds of ways. But, as the chapter shows, there is also a lot more to what makes rape stories believable. Ending the rape epidemic in South Africa is going to require that many more people think critically about how seemingly benign behaviour enables rape to thrive. In other words, we have to think unrelentingly about how what we are taught in patriarchal society – and all of us are brought up in such society – seduces us into thinking that rape only looks a certain way, and therefore that we should only believe rape when it fits into that very narrow idea.

I start this book with this memory of rapists on camera for various reasons. The programmes allow me to talk about some of the myths that accompany rape in the public consciousness. They also give me a chance to speak about rapists, something that is important, but that very often gets lost in our public gender talk. Although we have massive evidence that rape is a national sport, rapists themselves are often invisible in the public discourse on how to end rape. Everybody says we should raise our sons differently, and that is true. But we seldom reflect on how to shift public behaviour in today's adults, and even less on how we can individually – and collectively – sabotage rapists and hold them accountable. Instead, public discourse, with minority exceptions, proceeds as though focusing on rape survivors exclusively will end rape. It will not. This is the reminder in novelist Kagiso Lesego Molope's quotation in the epigraph. It is also the lesson at the heart of her extraordinary 2012 novel, *This Book Betrays My Brother*.

More importantly, when we recognise that rape is a huge problem in our society, we have to accept that something in our country enables it to happen. Something makes it acceptable for millions to get raped on a regular basis. That something is patriarchy. However, to say that patriarchy *enables* and *needs* rape culture can still be debilitating for many people who want to know what they can do to contribute to a significant decline in rape, and ultimately to the end of rape. But we can all contribute to a country that takes rape more seriously, that makes rapists less safe, and potential rapists to hesitate. We can ensure that there are consequences. I am not speaking about the law. Most of us can do little about the law, about forcing the criminal justice system to take rape seriously, so if that is the only consequence we imagine, we are not going to make much of a difference. Instead, we need to ask the hard questions and embark on the path that Helene Strauss gestures towards in the third epigraph to this book.

We often place so much pressure on women to talk about rape, to access counselling and get legal services to process rape, but very seldom do we talk about the rapists. We run the danger of speaking about rape as a perpetrator-less crime. Or speaking of rape as a crime with a perpetrator that is so strange, so foreign to our senses of what is human, that we cannot but be puzzled and rendered helpless to fight rape. Sometimes it feels as if aliens come down to Earth to rape those constructed as feminine and vulnerable, only to then jump back into their spaceships and return to their planet, leaving us shocked, brutalised and with inadequate technology to fight back, to make them stop, to hold them accountable or to act in collective self-defence.

For as long as we allow ourselves to talk about rape as a series of isolated, puzzling horrors that happen to women and children, we stop ourselves from really holding rapists accountable. We need to expand the ways in which we think about rape, and how to fight it. If something or some things in our society make rape possible, then we can change this. We are society.

This book is my contribution to that public conversation on how to curb rape and how to hold rapists accountable, how to understand this phenomenon that holds us hostage, and how to stop the cycles of complicity that keep us here. We need to confront the myths and excuses that enable rape, and I list and address some of these in Chapter 7. But there are more myths and I may not even have heard of some of them. You know what they are. And hopefully, as our collective thinking about rape shifts, we can all grow more alert to such myths. As I hope addressing them head-on demonstrates, these myths and excuses do dangerous work and often enable a rape culture.

Chapters 3 and 8 address post-apartheid South African public cultures that enable and make excuses for rape. Rape survives and flourishes in our country because it works and because there are very specific ways in which collective behaviours make it seem okay. While we cannot unmake history, we can directly confront those aspects of our current collective behaviour that support a rape culture. Violence of different kinds has a long history in our country as both assault and self-defence.

In Chapter 6, I look at child rapes, focusing on what is so striking about our responses to these. I argue that we often pretend that there are 'mild' rapes and 'brutal' rapes, terrible but 'understandable' rapes versus inexplicable and inexcusable rapes. When we do so, we often speak of the rapes of children and old women as the 'worst' kinds of rapes. Yet, they form part of the very fabric of rape in the country – they are neither rare nor different in their brutality. All rape is brutal. It is not possible to speak of some rapes as the worst without suggesting at the very least that some rapes are 'understandable'. But this system of gradation goes to the heart of the problem. It will never be possible to eliminate the rapes considered most brutal without dismantling what makes rape not just possible but also so permissible in our society. There is not much we can do about the past, but there is a wealth of different options in the present, if we are as seriously disturbed by rape as a society as we say we are. Furthermore, as Grace Musila's comments on this manuscript helped me better understand, there are overlaps between the designation of some rape as the 'worst' because they are enacted on the bodies of babies and old women, on the one hand, and 'curative'/'corrective' rape. Both kinds are defined by a shared logic of compulsory literal and symbolic availability of all women to male heterosexual pleasure. In other words, both the responses to the former and the existence of the latter draw from the taken-for-granted assumption that all women should literally and theoretically be available for the pleasure of heterosexual men. Crudely put, society raises us to believe that this is the function of women's bodies – to please men sexually and symbolically. This is why women are accused of overreacting when we are angered by public sexual harassment, codified as legitimate appreciation. It is because of this underlying assumption that heterosexual men's pleasure not only trumps our displeasure but that it nullifies our experience of unwanted attention as threatening.

Therefore the outrage at baby and elder rape is because these are children/women who lie outside the socially sanctioned bounds of sexual availability (because they are too young or too old), while 'curative'/'corrective' rape is about 'punishing' women who lie within the sexual eligibility window for heterosexual male consumption, but they 'dare' not to be available – hence the belief that they deliberately choose to make themselves 'unavailable' to male sexual gratification, and can therefore be punished and/or violently recovered.

If Chapter 6 brings together a string of case studies, then Chapter 5 deals with only one: the 2006 Jacob Zuma rape trial. I could have chosen other very high-profile cases to focus on. However, this case was a watershed moment and instructive on many levels. My approach to this trial is not so much what happened inside the court case, but rather how the trial also played out in the court of public opinion. At the time, many of us argued that there was much about this particular rape case that reflected what happens in many rape cases across the country. At the same time, because it happened on such a large scale, many of the responses were amplified, perhaps allowing us to see them differently and clearly.

I have another motive for using this trial – it offers me an opportunity to examine the significant outpouring of support for the woman at the centre of the case – named Khwezi, to protect her identity – by feminists who wrote in to national weeklies, while also allowing me to see how those who were featured in the papers as unconditionally supportive of the accused Jacob Zuma spoke about their support. In the global obsession with South Africa as rape capital, you would be forgiven for thinking that there is no contestation and no active fight against rape by feminists, whatever the risk. Yet, at least in the field of contemporary South African writing – poetry, memoir, fiction – there is enough material for various books on the relationship between rape and the post-apartheid feminist imagination. This chapter is one of the places where I look at specific collective feminist energies against rape in the public domain. The One in Nine Campaign provided the most consistent support for Khwezi. It was formed specifically by organisations and individual feminists to support Khwezi in what was clearly going to be a highly publicised traumatic experience for her. Even as attacks on her were anticipated, I doubt any of the founding feminists understood the sheer scale of what she would confront. And I say that even as most of these feminists had extensive experience in anti-rape and anti-violence activism and professional work. Nonetheless, One in Nine Campaign members stood firm in purple shirts in support of Khwezi against a sea of supporters who sometimes travelled from other parts of the country to support Zuma. The purple pavement is real, and it may not be a majority movement that brings cities to a standstill, but it is not going anywhere. For as long as there is rape, there will be feminists who will fight it. We believe it is a fight that we cannot opt out of even if we want to. You can try to avoid sleeping to prevent a recurring nightmare, but sooner or later the human body shuts you down and the nightmare returns. In any event, even when we are wide awake, a recurring nightmare retains its grip on us though fear, memory and certainty of its return. It cannot be avoided. It needs to be confronted. In One in Nine, like other feminists everywhere in the world, we know that women cannot be free for as long as rape exists in the world.

Before the Zuma rape trial, I was much more hopeful about our fight against rape as a society, even confronted by the statistics. I believed most people when they said they opposed rape, even though I was very aware of South African hypocrisy when it comes to gender power. After the trial, having witnessed what happened outside, how far people were willing to go to terrorise a woman in defence of a powerful man, it is clear to me that something drastic needs to change before this culture consumes us whole. The One in Nine Campaign does not believe in violence, disavowing violence as a patriarchal weapon, and I have agreed to be bound by this kind of feminism. But there are times when I wonder what would happen if women fought back in defence of ourselves, in numbers and unapologetically. When I read Angela Makholwa's superb novel *Black Widow Society*, the suspension of disbelief that works of fiction offer readers allowed me to entertain a different feminist position: one where women kill men who violate women, where women do so for themselves and in defence of one another. And there have been times when I have been convinced that the only reason the patriarchal siege continues unabated is because violent men know women will not rise up, take arms and collectively defend our own. It feels true sometimes. However, I also know that this does not make sense – everywhere in history there is evidence of people who defended themselves and broke regimes down yet globally white supremacy persists. Audre Lorde, whom a dear friend and sister prays to as "holy mother full of fire", reminds us that "the master's tools will not dismantle the master's house". Violence is the master's tool.

We need new tools, not in place of, but in *addition* to the current anti-violent strategies we have. Holding rapists accountable is a start. I am not saying that the young men on whose narratives I started this chapter were representative of rapists. They need not be. And, I am convinced that they are not. But they open the door to understanding how rape is possible: because to treat women as though they do not matter is deeply engrained in our culture as South Africans.

I will admit to being despondent about the state of violence against women in South Africa today. As I drive to work in the final days of writing this manuscript, all the radio shows are abuzz with news of Paralympian Oscar Pistorius being released on house arrest after serving only ten months for killing his girlfriend, Reeva Steenkamp. I cannot tune out the news of the fact that the Stutterheim rapist, farmer William Knoetze, was sentenced to fifteen years for repeatedly raping three girls. And I am unable to erase from my mind's eye the television news footage of a stone-faced former tennis superstar Bob Hewitt in court, nor his six-year sentence for raping a succession of girls. Perhaps he did not feel as nonchalant as he looked. With these and many other powerful, sometimes famous men in mind, I cannot accept the lie that poverty makes it more likely for men to rape. The image of poor, young Black men as the figures of the rapist is not the reality South African women live under. If that were so, then some groups of women would be safe when they lived lives that brought them into minimal contact with these men who are the face of the rapist in public discourse.

Rape is a crime of power, and in patriarchal societies, all men

11

can access patriarchal power. Wealthy white men like Knoetze and Hewitt rape and those like Pistorius kill their partners, as do wealthy Black men. Quibbling over the class of rapist is a distraction. It misses the point. It also excuses those men who are poor and Black, pretending that those among them who choose to rape cannot help themselves, that they are victims of circumstance.

It is not true that 'hurt people hurt people'.

Otherwise queer, working-class people of colour would be the most violent people on the planet.

It is condescending to poor people to suggest that these men cannot be held accountable for choosing to rape. It is also the most pernicious patriarchal lie that men – any men and all men — cannot help themselves when confronted by women's bodies. It is rape culture. Rape culture renders rape acceptable.

Rape is never mild, never minor, never acceptable. It is not just sex. The cost to survivors who speak out is so significant that it does not make sense to fabricate rape except as an exercise in self-immolation because in patriarchal society, the dominant response to a human being 'breaking the silence' is disbelief. Therefore, those people who constantly say "but women sometimes lie" are part of the problem. Each time someone says, hears and believes that most women lie about rape – or that saying so is the legitimate response to someone telling you that s/he or they were raped – they make it more unlikely that someone else will speak of their own violation.

It is not immediately clear to me whether violence against women is on the increase or not. What does seem clear is the manner in which it seems to be more brazen, and I am not sure whether it is being reported more directly in the news and therefore more visible in its brazenness or whether there has been an upward turn. Given the fact that rape-reporting numbers are always much lower than incidents of rape, this is not a question we can confidently answer in the short term.

One thing is very clear to me about the numbers and statistics. In the immediate aftermath of April 1994, rape-charge statistics rose, not because rape increased in a new country, but because women felt more likely to be believed. We all believed that political power would make this possible, that freedom would mean that the police force and the criminal justice system would belong to us too. Many Black women would not have gone to a police station to report rape as readily under apartheid, whether their rapists were white or Black. Nothing about apartheid made Black women feel valued or taken seriously. Apartheid law treated women as minors who could not make any significant decisions in their own names, not even enter a contract for themselves. It punished those women who entered professional life for getting married, such as the fact that Black women teachers would lose their access to permanent employment as soon as they were married, exposing them to increasing vulnerability if the marriage did not work. Sindiwe Magona's autobiographies *To my children's children/Kubantwana babantwana bam* and *Forced to grow* are an incredible illustration of what could happen when a woman teacher plummets into poverty because she is married and her husband has abandoned her and their children. Magona's autobiographies are worth reading for many more reasons, in addition to these.

At the same time, women activists' autobiographies are rife with examples of how frequently sexual violence, rape and the threat of rape were used as a form of torture. How could women then trust police officers – some of whom had this approach to rape, and some of whom were proud rapists themselves – to do anything for them when they had been raped by non-policemen?

All of these problems are when talking about Black women who have been raped by Black men. Why would most white women raped by white men lay charges against them with police officers in a white supremacist patriarchal system that not only made white women minors themselves, but also constructed the cruel myth that white men could not rape? And what hope could Black women raped by white men have in an apartheid legal justice system?

Finally, given the constant active onslaught that apartheid was to Black life, policestations were not exactly a place we (as Black people) wanted to be anywhere near for any reason. In this context, many women felt that laying charges against Black men in such a system would render them complicit with the system. Here the

13

choice was not a choice at all: handing over another Black person to a brutal racist state or placing your own vulnerability in the hands of a brutal racist state. This was not a state that invited confidence.

For vulnerable people who were not women, reporting rape also meant dealing with the kind of incomprehension and humiliation that comes with masculinist culture, such as the questioning of a man's own masculinity in not being able to defend himself against another man's violation. Rape is an exercise of patriarchal violent power against those who are safe to violate: mostly women, girls and boys but also adult men and trans-people deemed safe to violate. Queer desire and gender non-conformity were explicitly criminalised and policed in apartheid South Africa, thereby further dissuading gay men and transgender individuals from reporting rape.

Of course, many people fought all of these doubts and reported rape under apartheid, and their courage is remarkable. However, the hope that came with the end of apartheid and the ushering in of a new democracy that spoke directly about undoing not just racial oppression but also taking women seriously, and recognising the necessity of celebrating the full spectrum of gender and sexual rights, saw people's confidence in the state soar. It is therefore not surprising that rape survivors expected that the post-1994 criminal justice system could offer them justice.

This dream and hope, however, was to be betrayed again and again from 1994. Rape survivors who have not already learnt this lesson will most likely do so if the current system remains unchanged. Many others also know that justice for most survivors of rape does not lie in the criminal justice system, and in fact, it may lie nowhere. Thus under-reporting to police will continue to be a feature. In South Africa, the Medical Research Council reported in 2005 that only one in nine women who are raped report it to the police. The other eight deal with their rape differently. Their mistrust of the criminal justice system is clear as they seek medical, counselling and other assistance to deal with their trauma, to find healing, resolution and sometimes justice. We will never know how many survivors remain silent foregoing assistance of any kind.

Many of us try to understand why rape is such a big part of South

African contemporary life, and why it may be on the rise. Speaking as one of the panelists at the 2013 Thabo Mbeki Foundation's International Women's Day event, themed "OAU@50: Women at the Centre of Development: Celebrating women's progress", Thenjiwe Mtintso spoke about this relentless policing and violence as a crisis. The crisis, she argued, is the latest form of the backlash. In other words, it is a direct attempt to undo feminist work and gains. Yes, it is the 'usual' patriarchal violence in many senses. But it is also a patriarchy defending itself. It is not a coincidence that South African women, who, on paper are so empowered and have won so many freedoms, are living with the constant fear of violence when we cross the street, at work, everywhere. An effective backlash always does much more than neutralise gains, though; it reverses the gains we see everywhere and it reminds those who might benefit from such gains that they are not quite free. We can see the same thing in the US with a Black president and the constant violence by police and others on Black children and adults carried across the globe in news headlines. The sheer magnitude also makes us wonder about how much more violence goes unreported. It also creates a culture of instability and fear that reminds African Americans that they are not free and that they will pay for each gain. It is not new violence, and its targets are not just African Americans but Latinos, Latinas and Native Americans too, although the headlines do not always travel as far across the globe. The rape backlash that Mtintso speaks about proceeds along the same lines: it is not new, but it is more brazen. It is a critical time for feminists who already are so stretched and strained in this part of the world and continent.

In the midst of this backlash, public shaming and a criminal justice system that betrays them, women are repeatedly invited to break the silence. There is no silence. We know we live in the midst of a rape crisis.

It is time to apply pressure on men who rape, those who make excuses for rapists, those who make rape 'jokes', and to pressure our government to create a criminal justice system that works to bring the possibility of justice to rape survivors and all other survivors of violence. The silence we must now break is the silence around the identities of the rapists in our midst. It is no longer acceptable – or convincing – to pretend that men who rape women, children and other men are a small fringe minority of men we do not know. Most survivors know their rapists. It is simply not possible for a small minority of men to hold a country hostage in this way. And if it is, then we know who that minority is, so they need to be stopped.

It is also important for men who choose not to rape to stop being complicit and sometimes directly undermining attempts to end rape culture. Men who are not violent need to stop responding angrily to those who seek to end rape, accusing us of blaming all men, and requiring that we start by saying "not all men". Men who do not rape have nothing to be ashamed of when rapists are held accountable. And they need to direct their anger at the men who make all of them 'look bad'. They need to confront the men who rape and create rape culture, and stop sabotaging those who engage in a fight to end rape by insisting that any critique of endemic rape be prefaced with "not all men rape".

For many survivors of violence, the only thing the criminal justice system offers is secondary victimisation. There are several examples in this book. There are millions upon millions more in the real world. It is crucial to focus on survivors and victims as we do in the work that tries to find healing and justice. It is also crucial to be honest about what we know, to render visible/audible what is obscured, but also to pay attention to the many meanings of silence, especially when they point to the limitations of litigation. There is no doubt that all of these feminist ways of thinking about violence have been invaluable.

But they also offer an opportunity to rethink our feminist work, especially when we think about the gains of such work. It is a success that feminist work has made it impossible for people to claim progressive politics without pledging commitment to anti-patriarchal ideas. Yet, we have not been able to move this beyond lip service in a society where men are routinely rewarded for being violent with better or unaffected career trajectories, loyalties and self-appointed armies coming to their defence. So, as in that much cited poem by Roshila Nair, a poem that I insert into Chapter 2 in this book, we need to break the cycles on hypocrisy. In South Africa, men acquire more kudos for speaking non-sexism and even feminism, but they still go home and act in misogynist ways with no real cost.

In recent years, there has been the establishment of a women's Ministry, calling for President Zuma to fund an inquiry on gendered violence, to speak more strongly against rape. What does this call, this expectation, even creating this possibility, do? I understand that part of this is getting the president of the Republic to put money and resources in place so that anti-patriarchal work can happen further. What does it mean to ask this president to take anti-rape work seriously, after we lived through the brutalisation of Khwezi in more than one way? What does it mean for this to even be a call, and/or a reality, especially for those of us who believe Khwezi?

Jacob Zuma was acquitted of rape by a court of law, and those who call on him to make funds available, and to take a tougher stance against rape and other gendered violence point to this. However, whatever the court found, it did not absolve his refusal to limit the levels of brutality that happened in his name. When his followers terrorised Khwezi and her supporters, he did nothing to temper this even though they did it in his name. How do you think the millions of women who are rape survivors, who were raped by various men in 2006 felt watching what happens to women who speak out and those that support them?

Ending rape is going to require that we interrupt all the narratives of rape culture. It requires honesty about the fact that there are systems that support rape culture and that the ways in which we support rape survivors matters. I understand the sentiments behind wearing a certain colour – black or white – in solidarity with rape survivors. I wonder what it would mean if most of us required more of ourselves. While I also understand the symbolic value of walking in heels, possibly getting blisters in marches that show solidarity with the pain of living with patriarchal expectation, I wonder whether the message does not get lost in the fun and humour of such marches. More significantly, whether it does not allow us to go home and rest on our laurels because we did our bit to end violence. I am not knocking marches. That would be foolhardy, as would knocking people's attempts to do something, to publicly announce that they are committed to ending violence. I am merely asking why we don't do more that does not even require that we drive somewhere else: why we look away when a woman is attacked in public, why we avert our gaze when a gay man is mocked in our presence, why we say nothing when someone we know comments violently on someone else, diminishing them in the process.

In addition to the current strategies of marches and protests, we need to find new ways to make violent men unsafe and to end the impunity with which they enact violence. Many aspects of our public gender talk need revisiting. Many forms of violence happen in plain sight and sometimes with the active complicity of spectators. What are we saying to survivors of sexual assault when we ask them to break the silence even though we avert our gaze when other forms of violence and humiliation of people happen in our presence?

How can we shift our perspectives and behaviour in ways that make it harder for violence to happen in our presence? How can we render violators unsafe? Why is it that most of us look away even when the violators are in the minority and audiences in the majority?

Recently, in a conversation where we spoke about rape as endemic, and where we spoke about the routine abuse of school children by paedophiles in positions of power, one of my friends asked a question that caused us all to pause.

She asked, "What do we mean? What are you saying when you say it happened all the time in school?"

Think about that question for a minute before reading on. It is not as simple as it seems.

How we speak about and respond to violence matters. "It happens all the time" points to the crisis, debunking the myth that it is shocking and expressed in isolated incidents. That phrasing also suggests that it is commonplace, normal: "All the time". It happens. The truth is that it does not just 'happen'. Individuals *choose* to rape and they make this choice because it is an available one, and one that is mostly without consequence to themselves.

But there is a cost – a huge, devastating cost that comes with rape – an invisible wound that remains long after the physical scars (where these exist) have healed. And what a cost to us to have so many of our people walking wounded.

As a society, we can do so much better.

CHAPTER 1

A recurring nightmare

Rape is not a South African invention. Nor is it distasteful sex. It is sexualised violence, a global phenomenon that exists across vast periods in human history. Rape has survived as long as it has because it works to keep patriarchy intact. It communicates clearly who matters and who is disposable. Those who matter are not afraid of being raped because they have not been taught to fear sexual assault. They have been taught safety. Rape is the communication of patriarchal power, reigning in, enforcing submission and punishing defiance. It is an extreme act of aggression and of power, always gendered and enacted against the feminine. The feminine may not always be embodied in a woman's body; it may be enacted against a child of any gender, a man who is considered inappropriately masculine and any gender non-conforming people. Rape has also been central to the spread of white supremacy, and to the way race and racism have organised the world over the last four hundred years.

Rape is something we have come to expect from areas of conflict, a threat we are adept at deciphering and a nightmare regularly reported on in our media. It appears everywhere: in a political speech about decolonisation as the legitimate response against the rape of the continent/land, repeatedly as something that happens to women who are out of control but need to be checked, as constitutive of *swaartgevaar*, as one of the constitutive elements of societies structured on slavery (slavocratic societies), as something that can be easily denied, as conspiracy, on the placard of an orange overall-clad Police and Prisons Civil Rights Union (POPCRU) leader and South African Prisoners Organisation for Human Rights (SAPOHR) president Golden Miles Bhudu declaring the accused in a rape case as 'raped', in a Zapiro cartoon where 'lady justice' lies prone as the tri-partite alliance get ready to rape her, and as one of the reasons why a Minister with a record of gender progressive activism storms out of an exhibition by ten Black women artists.

This book is called *Rape: a South African nightmare* because although rape is part of our contemporary gender talk, our constant preoccupation with it plays itself out as a series of miscommunications and missed opportunities. In other words, although we talk about it all the time, read about, and fight against it, we cannot make it go away. It is an enigma in post-apartheid South Africa since very few admit to being rapists, yet millions are raped each year. As our newspapers cover more and more instances of rape, we respond to them as individual acts of brutality, as we must in order to be empathetic to the violated, but, having done that, we then stop short of reading rape as more than a moment, a singular event. Every time we read a rape as an isolated, enigmatic event, we move further away from curbing the alarming statistics, interrupting the patterns and transforming gender power. And so the nightmare recurs with largely similar responses replayed.

By looking at different aspects of rape and rape talk in South Africa, across epochs, I make the assertion that rape is not a moment but a language, and in the pages that follow I untangle and decipher the knots and codes of this language, to surface its structure, underline its histories, understand its rules, pore over its syntax, page through its dictionaries, vocabularies and what it communicates. I am indebted to a substantial body of writing on rape as I do so, revisiting some of these arguments made about rape, asking questions about why rape often works in ways that seem counterintuitive. I am not interested in writing a bible on rape, nor in merely distilling here what the patterns are in rape research. I limit the public discussions I analyse to South African ones, not because I think there is nothing to be learnt from elsewhere, or because South Africa is exceptional, but to probe specific relationships to rape, specific histories of rape, surface our blindspots and to better reflect on possible ways out of the quagmire.

This is a political project. I am invested in trying to figure out how we can change collective approaches to rape from different spaces and how to broaden transformative praxis beyond the small radical healing and generative spaces of organisations opposed to gendered violence. The personal and political motivation for this book comes from the same place as the sense of unfairness my friends and I felt when we were young and when girls were humiliated, sexually harassed, slut-shamed and molested, the same place that motivated my training and volunteer work as a Rape Crisis counsellor two decades ago, and the same place that prompted my membership of the One in Nine Campaign, an organisation that takes a multi-layered approach to feminist anti-rape work.

When I did the bulk of my work at Rape Crisis Observatory and Khayelitsha, I was also writing a Master's thesis on the first five years of *Staffrider* magazine. I had been ill-prepared for the space that raped fictional Black women characters occupied in those short stories, and had I known I may have chosen an entirely different research project. I've written in that thesis and elsewhere about how to make sense of the fact that almost a third of the stories published in this literary magazine contained a Black woman character raped by a white man character. I tried to understand the relationship between, on the one hand, the fact that rape was clearly violence that these women characters could not escape in the hands of brutal white men characters, and the fact that it was only those Black women characters who defied their societies' prescriptions on appropriate feminine behaviour that were raped in these stories, on the other hand. It was clear that rape was being written as punishment for bad behaviour, and it was also clear that the rape of Black women by white men was a constant preoccupation for these writers. For two years, I pored over, and tried to make sense of this preoccupation with rape in the magazine. It was intellectual work but it was also emotionally distressing reading and analysis. I wrote mostly in the early mornings and late at night. During the day I went to my paid and volunteer work: in the morning I mostly went to my part-time tutoring jobs in the English Department and Academic Development Programme at UCT as well as Academic Development Unit in what was then Cape Technikon, all work that brought me enormous joy. For a few hours a week, I counselled rape survivor clients at Rape Crisis. Very difficult work, I nonetheless found counselling enormously rewarding and healing because sometimes a girl or woman moved through trauma to hope, and also because many of the women who were similarly volunteering were the most remarkable people I have ever met. Their courage, dedication and support was another affirmation of feminist community, not my first, but one that changed me nonetheless.

At the same time, there was not much I was able to do when a friend of mine was abducted and gang raped, when she reported the crime, refused any kind of counselling, and had the successfully collected evidence of her rapists used against her in court. We were starting to be very aware of HIV, and when she realised they were going to rape her, she had pleaded with them to use a condom. In the end, although her body bore the kind of evidence of physical and sexual attack that our society expects to see in typical rape cases, she led the police officers to the site of her rape where the condoms were collected in evidence, and she had provided enough information to get the rapists arrested, various legal justice officials pointed out to her that the fact that the men had used condoms on her prompting meant she had consented. Her boyfriend begged me every day to convince her to go for counselling, and my then boyfriend tried hard to understand what I meant when I said it was not right to pressure her into anything. I recognised their frustration, but knew that she needed to feel strong, not weak;

I believed her when she said to me that she did not need help. In *Teaching my mother how to give birth,* Kenyan-born Somali poet Warsan Shire reminds us that "sometimes the wound is by the healer" even with the best of intentions, and the Rape Crisis training had affirmed a principle I had learnt quite early on in my feminism: that each woman's process is different and forcing solutions is not empowering.

It was at about this time, as I wrote about rape for my thesis, counselled my clients and battled with how to support my most recent rape survivor friend, that I was discovering and falling in love with Miriam Tlali. I thought I was drawn to her because she was a Black feminist who had written consistently throughout the 1980s: a column, essays, interviews with other women writers trying to make sense of the relationships between Black women and writing, novels and short stories. I loved that when she wrote about rape she did so differently from her peers, with gentleness and empathy for her women characters, told from their perspectives. As a reader, I was delighted by the dialogue she wrote into her characters' mouths.

In the story "Devil at a dead end" from her 1989 collection of short stories, *Footprints in the Quag*, Miriam Tlali's unnamed girl narrator escapes rape by outsmarting the lecherous white clerk who sneaks into her carriage when she is alone and asleep, by telling him she is "afflicted with a venereal sickness", using the word "*makoala*". Tlali's narrator notices:

> The impact of that word was quick, merciless, shocking and immediately disarming. Like when in a dark alley you suddenly grope into a dead end. She stood still listening to the sound of receding breath. She reached below the bunk above and lowered the dim switch. She watched the recoiling devilish figure and drew a sigh of relief.

Unable to physically resist her assailant, this young woman outsmarts him by doing with her mind what her body has failed to do. In another story that appears earlier in the collection,

"Fud-u-u-a!", women unsuccessfully try to escape groping and rape in congested train conditions, and build a community as one of the ways to defend themselves.

Unlike the stories I was writing about in my thesis, Tlali's girls and women understand, analyse and develop ways to deal with the threats, fear and experience of rape, collectively and individually; they believe, help and protect one another. They are not just bodies and metaphors, not just faces and vaginas, their bodies are not battlegrounds. Instead, she repeatedly made different choices for her characters whether they feared, escaped or survived rape. They were never deviant outsiders written as though they deserved what had happened to them because of their foolishness or transgressions. They belong to a community of women who protect and fight alongside one another.

Each reading of Tlali offers the possibility that something might be illuminated differently, a reminder that some solutions require taking the imagination seriously. Writing and imagining is doing – it is action and politically consequential, not retreat. Tanzanian literary scholar Susan Andrade insists that we should think about African feminist work in terms of what is generated by *rioting women* and *writing women*, not as oppositional but complementary. For Andrade, rioting/writing women are political, practical, imaginative, and both are the birthplaces of intellectual abstraction. Following Andrade, I like to think that sometimes writing women *are* rioting women.

A few years ago, when I first encountered this essay, it aptly captured the substantial thinking, strategising and analysis that I had encountered in activist spaces and significantly challenged the dominant academic frames that pretended that abstraction happened among those located in institutional spaces designated intellectual, whereas activist spaces exhibited only practice. I think many of us who came to feminism before we entered university research careers know this: that some of the most transformative, thought-provoking abstraction is taught in activist communities not in classrooms. In the One in Nine Campaign, for example, the textures of thinking, reflection, debate and discussion that go into every campaign of direct action remind me of this constantly.

This is the context of writing this book for me. From this context, I want to ask questions about the society I am part of and its relationships to rape. Writing is also thinking and rethinking some of these questions. It exists alongside conversations with other feminists in community and individually.

If South Africans generally are opposed to rape, then why does it continue to be such a huge part of everyday life, with so few interventions? Why is rape so often met with disbelief, second-guessing and invitations to keep it under wraps? Why are some rapes perceived as more shocking and devastating than others? What does it mean to invite survivors to break the silence, report and lay charges against rapists when successful prosecution rates are so low?

After one of my op-eds on the Jacob Zuma rape trial had been published by a national paper in 2006, an old friend called me to express concern that I might be read as "not just as feminist but also a rape survivor". For my friend, although the former was perfectly acceptable since it was a deliberate political stance, the latter was worrisome because, as he argued, it might delegitimise and stigmatise me. As I pointed out to him, there is something wrong with a society that stigmatises survivors, and dissuades others from supporting them publicly and privately rather than shaming the perpetrators. It was equally perverse that survivors could be dissuaded from speaking in support of one another, and against rape culture. I did not understand then what it meant to be a feminist who bit her tongue on rape. I still do not.

The question that has replayed on a loop since I received that phone call, however, is: how could being a survivor disqualify a person from speaking against rape?

This suggestion seemed as counterintuitive to me as my friend's stated concern. This friend was the kind of man who actively worked for greater women's representation on various leadership structures in his movement, someone who had often been the sole man repeatedly arguing for the recognition of sexual harassment as violence in his organisation, and that unfashionable person who not only intervened when a man beat his girlfriend at a party, but also once broke a neighbour's door down in order to assist the woman screaming in pain inside. He was the kind of man women consider an ally.

He has never asked me whether I was in fact a rape survivor. He readily assumed that if I was, he would have known. I asked him how a non-survivor feminist's opposition to rape retained legitimacy when a feminist who was also a rape survivor would be disqualified. My ambivalence about this conversation notwithstanding, it illustrates something about many people's responses to rape.

When I asked my friend whether he believed Khwezi, he responded without hesitation that he did. When I asked him whether he thought she deserved support, he responded similarly. What struck me as counterintuitive about my friend's concern was how those with experience were least qualified to speak against rape. In most other contexts, intimate familiarity with a subject and an experience raises you above those with less direct contact. We live in a global culture that reminds us that experience is the best teacher, where having gone through something not only makes you worth listening to, but also builds careers. Bestseller lists are brimming with books penned by authors who have bounced back from bankruptcy to attain affluence, offering advice on how to also acquire wealth. We listen attentively to experts who have studied phenomena as they explain to us how things work, and help us make sense of what is in front of us. Everywhere I looked, people who knew what they were talking about were celebrated. We think of first-hand accounts as more reliable than second-hand ones, make witnesses indispensable to fact-finding missions and court processes alike.

But none of this applies to the testimony of those who have survived rape.

My friend was right. The dominant script on rape inverts the usual expectations. When a rape survivor speaks of her own rape, she is only generally believable under very narrow circumstances. When she speaks about rape inflicted on another, she is assumed unreliable because she is too emotionally invested, 'biased' – too quick to believe rape is widespread. It is not empathy, recognition or knowledge that is assumed. It is a form of paranoia. If the rape survivor's own rape was disbelieved, speaking in solidarity with another is also dismissed.

Jane Bennett's research shows how the believability of a rape survivor depends on how closely her rape resembles her society's idea of what a rape looks like, who rapes, who can be raped, when and how. In other words, every time a woman says she has been raped, whether we believe her or not depends on what we believe about what rape looks like. The closer her story is to our preconceived ideas about what rape looks like, the more likely we are to believe she is telling the truth.

When feminists insist, as we must, that rape is violence and not sex, this information is filtered through lenses that cast violence in physical ways. Commonsensical understandings of violence often assume it will leave a 'physical' imprint on the body: a bruise, blood, a broken bone. A visibly injured or broken body provides a form of 'proof' of coercion, allowing the listener to turn away from the story told by the survivor to the body of the survivor. The story told by a woman needs a body of evidence. It is not an interest in the pain of the rape, but a burden of proof placed on the survivor or victim of the rape. Jane Bennett speaks about what it means to live "within and across the failures of language" because rape is not only violence enacted on and against the body with an external weapon that leaves the kind of proof often expected. Sometimes rape leaves bruises on skin, cuts, tears. Sometimes it leaves invisible scars only. The body that seems whole, then, can work against the experience of violation narrated by the violated woman.

Bennett explains that women's stories of rape are believed or doubted based on the relationship between plausibility and credibility. This is true inside and outside court.

When a rape closely resembles what the hearer expects a rape to look like, then the survivor's tale is plausible. Plausibility is about, and dependent on, the hearer and what that hearer deems possible; it is not about the specific person speaking. Bennett writes:

> [t]he plausibility of a story in itself is a function of its hearer's readiness to make sense of its organisation at multiple levels: the plausibility of narrative relies on the symbiotic relation of text organization (schemas) and cultural assumptions about the way the world works.

In other words, plausibility depends on a range of things all of which are dependent on the audience of the narrated events. The listener/reader has to: firstly, be open to believing and understanding what is presented; secondly, find that the different events and aspects of what is being told individually make sense; thirdly, be convinced of the connections between said events/aspects of the narrated rape; and finally, everything together has to be possible in how the listener/reader thinks the world works. A rape story is plausible when all four requirements are consistent.

Let me illustrate.

When a teacher listens to a crying student narrate her rape, the latter's story's plausibility depends on the teacher believing that the torn skirt, dirty shirt, and unruly soiled hair and cut lip of the student in front of her are valid signs of the student's struggle and violation. The student's body looks like she has been attacked. The teacher has to believe each of the events are logical, that their sequence makes sense and that the student's way of telling them is logical. The correlation between what the teacher sees and hears is seamless. The teacher also has to believe that in the world, girls are sometimes pulled into the bushes by boys, that boys from a competing school are thugs, and that when girls are in pain, they cry. The student's story is coherent in itself, her body backs up what she says, and what she tells her teacher is possible in the world.

This plausibility is disrupted if any of these elements are missing. Bennett reminds us that when survivors present a story that meets expectations of the audience, such plausibility often increases the likelihood of a guilty verdict in court cases.

In other words, what Bennett is saying here is that inside and outside courts across different countries, what is accepted as plausible is that which confirms preconceived ideas about what rape is, who rapes, when, who gets raped, when and how. Therefore, when we live in societies that hold onto the view that those likely to rape look and sound a certain way, which is clearly defined as very different from how those who can be raped look, we may find specific narration of rape plausible. Plausibility relies on the construction of rapist-potential, what Bennett calls "a strongly about-to-be-rapist" and the consistency of the combined picture of who says she was raped and her narrative, or "momentary steadiness".

In addition to plausibility, credibility is required. Plausibility is about the listener, whereas credibility is about the person telling the story of the rape. Credibility depends on how believable the speaker is. To be believable, the speaker has to fall into a category that is seen as possible-to-rape; it has to be someone who can be raped. Not all people are seen as possible-to-rape. Sex workers, wives, slave women and men are all categories of people that have at different stages been placed in the category of 'impossible-to-rape'. This does not mean that nobody raped them. It means that when they were sexually violated, it was not recognised as such, legally and socially. People who are placed in the category 'impossible-to-rape' are routinely disbelieved when they report rape.

Because societal attitudes to rape continue to frame it as a kind of inappropriate sex, sex workers/prostitutes have a harder time convincing people they have been raped. Sex workers belong to a group marked as 'impossible-to-rape'. This is because of what they do for a living and patriarchal attitudes to women who have sex. In other words, many people assume that sex workers/prostitutes need to have insatiable appetites for sexual intercourse in order to work daily, and because women's sexual appetites are already always policed, this perceived desire/capacity for abundant sex is seen as deviant. The argument often then follows that if sexually deviant, they are always ready to have sex, and therefore cannot say no. They are impossible to rape in this argument because they are always willing to have sex.

There are many problems with this line of argument and all of them require conflation and avoidance to build a seemingly logical argument. In the minds of many, prostitution is about excessive, deviant sex, not a paid service. Consequently, patriarchal ideas about women who have uncontained sex spill over into readings of women sex workers. This disapproval of women who have 'deviant' sex also occludes the difficult and sometimes coercive routes to prostitution. Failure to see sex work/prostitution as work means that it is denied the basic assumptions we accord to all other paid services: choice over whom to transact with, thereby conflating sex for money/pleasure and rape. Sex workers/prostitutes are deemed impossible to rape because they are constructed as always willing to have sex with anybody. They cannot say no. Furthermore, because they are deviant and criminalised, they are not reliable witnesses.

In many societies in the world, religion and law insist that a man is entitled to sex with his wife, and that even when this is forced sex, it cannot be rape. This entitlement, often called 'conjugal rights' is also loaded with assumptions about women's sexual appetites, control of their own bodies and the proper place for heterosexual sex. Just as women with sexual appetites that do not conform to ideal patriarchal femininity are policed and sometimes stigmatised, women who will not have sex in marriage are faulted. If men are entitled to 'conjugal rights', then women owe their husbands sex. Fortunately, South African law recognises marital rape, but it is not free from the difficulties that haunt all other categories of rape.

Credibility is therefore already in question when a sex worker/ prostitute or wife reports rape.

Credibility also relies very heavily on the believability of who she says raped her. The accused has to fall into a category of potential rapist; strangers, poor men, Black men, socially inept men are seen as potential rapists. Powerful, popular, successful men are often excluded from the category of potential rapist.

This is why when women accuse powerful, famous and popular men of rape, so many people find this unbelievable even if they have no personal relationship with either accused rapist or the woman laying the charge. This was certainly the case with the

Jacob Zuma trial, since people who admired Zuma often could not reconcile the idea of the political figure that they had in their heads with what Khwezi was accusing him of. Before this, the same was evident in some public responses to Makhaya Ntini and after this to Zwelinzima Vavi.

When South African cricketer Makhaya Ntini was convicted of raping twenty-two-year-old Nomangezi Matokazi, and later freed on appeal, she was accused of being part of a plot to bring him down. He was powerful and at the top of his cricketing game, a hero, and therefore assumed to have access to any number of women sex partners. She was his opposite: a student who worked as a domestic worker. In a world where various idioms declare that the more affluent the man, the higher his capacity to attract women, her narrative did not make sense. Women 'like her' are supposed to find 'men like him' irresistible.

In "The agony of a hero's victim" – her interview published in *City Press*, where she wanted to be named and photographed, hence my decision to name her here – Ms Matokazi demonstrated keen awareness of what determined whether strangers believed her or not, when she said:

> I want those who do not believe me to hear my whole story. My story is that Ntini raped me. Some people think I was sent by Boers to accuse Ntini of rape so he could be left out of the cricket team. That is not true. I don't want any of his money. All I want is for justice to be done and for him to be sent to jail for what he has done to me. I have lost my job and am no longer studying. My mother is on a farm in Idutywa with no one to support her. The way things are going with things getting lost [the investigating officers lost her notebooks], it looks like Ntini will win the case. There is nothing I can do. I don't trust men any longer. One can never tell what their intentions are. I trusted Ntini and look what he did to me. I never thought he would do this.

Contrary to the accusations that she has manufactured a rape tale for money, Matokazi declares her disinterest in his money; she has not been paid by any others for her testimony. Rather than enrichment, her life has been disrupted. She is interested only in a form of justice as acknowledgement of the harm inflicted on her.

Ntini is an over-achiever, arguably one of South Africa's greatest cricketers ever. He is easy to admire and often appears charming in interviews. In the same interview, Matokazi speaks of how he would often be seen playing with children, had always been nice and so she was not taken aback when he offered to drive her to the shops in the rain. It was an act of kindness that was consistent with her experience of him.

Fast bowler extraordinaire, Ntini is a Black cricketer in the highly racialised South African sports scene, one of the pioneers who exceeded our expectations. He is the young man we were rooting for and who was making us proud, but also a young man we had grown protective of because of the usual racist narrative that trivialises Black achievement.

It was therefore 'easy' for many to immediately jump to his defence, and to accuse Matokazi of being for sale. It was equally easy for racists who wanted Ntini left out of the cricket team because they are opposed to transformation in South African sport to believe Ntini capable of rape. Interestingly, although these two positions seem at odds, they also have something very significant in common: neither one is interested in Matokazi's experience. Her charge simply confirms pre-existing stances. For the pro-Ntini camp, her testimony offers another barrier for him to be supported and one that he has to overcome. For the racists, it confirms pre-existing stereotypes of Black men's bestiality which can be brought out to deligitimise his sporting prowess.

Both these narratives are directly confronted in her interview. Bennett shows that while what makes a story plausible often relies on stereotypes about the accused rapist, stereotypes about the group to which a survivor belongs very often work against her believability (credibility). In the examples above, and because people continue to think about rape as inappropriate sex, rather than as violence, powerful, popular men are not potential rapists because they have a large pool of willing, available, obligation-free sex. Gender talk is often peppered with assertions that members of this group do not need to rape; they do not need to force anyone to have sex with them when they have so many more options. For racists, the stereotype of the Black man as rapist makes Matokazi's story plausible.

Yet, there is another way to understand the relationships of powerful men to rape. If all men already possess patriarchal power, and can therefore choose to rape, then powerful men assume the position of supermen. Supermen's unfettered access to many anonymous women sexual partners can enhance the sense of entitlement to women's bodies and therefore resorting to violence to forcibly access it. Supermen know that many will come to their defence against any such allegations, and that their supporters will compare the woman's social standing with the man's and, finding her wanting, will ask "if he can have anyone he likes, why would he force you *of all people*?" This is an impossible question to answer.

Nobody wins against a hero.

Indeed, even in cases where various women emerge to accuse the same popular man of rape, many will prefer to pontificate over possible conspiracies than pay attention to the mounting evidence.

Credibility, then, continues to be a difficult issue for rape complainants. Conventional gender talk seeks to either hold a survivor responsible for her own rape or requires that she can tell a story that shows her total innocence. Innocence is almost impossible to prove, especially for adults. To be innocent, she needs to not be an adult woman. Bennett argues a woman narrating her rape has to create her own social credibility in ways that are oxymoronic: presenting a story that harmonises with notions of the 'typical' rape in her society and demonstrating levels of steadiness in her narrative that are almost impossible to attain. Pregs Govender had written in 2006:

In South Africa 2006 … [a] woman who has sex is a whore, a *hoor*, a prostitute – who like wives, cannot be raped. They are objects owned by men, whose bodies do not belong to them. Khwezi is

31 years old. At 31 very few, except nuns, yogis celibate since childhood or the Virgin Mary, can claim to have no sexual history. The message being conveyed is that if any woman or child decides to lay a charge of rape, this is how she will be crucified.

Govender is not writing about Matokazi here, although what she says is equally relevant. Women's sexual histories and general life experiences render them hard to believe because they are not innocent. At the time that both Matokazi and Khwezi testified, sexual history was permissible as part of the court proceedings. As Govender shows, contrary to popular opinion, reporting rape and going through the criminal justice system channels places women at further risk, rather than promising relief.

Like Bennett, Govender shows the impossibility of the expectations placed on those who report rape. Any sexual history complicates – and at times nullifies – her story of rape. Referring specifically to the legal treatment of women who report rape, Navi Pillay cautions "[i]n the eyes of the law, a woman is both Eve and Eva. As a pure, fragile female she must be specially protected; as a seductive sex object, from whom men must be protected. In both cases women are the victims", thereby driving home the manner in which the attitudes outlined in this chapter are not merely societal but those that resonate with legal treatment of rape complainants as well.

I believe an end to rape is both possible and worth fighting for. Given the range of ways in which the violation and interpretation of rape work in counterintuitive ways, as various chapters show, I suspect that we need to be especially imaginative to decrease the instances of rape, to change how we think rape works and to make it harder to rape.

CHAPTER 2

What's race got to do with rape?

There is a very simple answer to the question posed in the title of this chapter. And there is also a longer way to demonstrate that answer. The simple answer is: everything. The idea of race as a way of seeing, defining, experiencing and ordering the world is a fairly recent one in human history, and it draws extensively on the creation of sexual difference and sexual violence. Race as an idea becomes first, a form of knowledge and ordering system, which is then institutionalised thus gaining legitimacy through the extensive use of sexual violence. The history of race is the history of slavery, colonialism and race science. The various disciplines in the academy that rescue race from an idea and elevate it to a valid ordering and meaning-making system rely on sexual violence, sexual cataloguing and measuring the bodies of the enslaved and colonised. In this sense, empire is a pornographic project, as George Lamming and David Dabydeen suggest. To call empire pornographic is to highlight the manner in which the project of empire is sexually violent and spectacular (exaggerated) in its demonstration of power. It is therefore not possible to talk about the development of a language or race without talking about sexual violence. Race was made through rape in very direct, deliberate and indirect ways, as I will show.

Critically acclaimed Kenyan feminist activist, poet and theatre practitioner, Shailja Patel reminds us that when "you want to understand how power works in any society, watch who is carrying the shame and who is doing the shaming".

Patel is spot on. Shame is a function of oppression; it has everything to do with who is valued and who is invisibilised in any society. Although logically, it would seem to follow that those who have something to be ashamed of, that those who behave badly should feel ashamed of themselves, the opposite is true. Shame is the product of dehumanisation, and all systems of violent oppressive power produce shame in those they brutalise. Therefore, when Patel speaks of following the paths of shame as a reliable predictor of power, she points to shame as an expression of trauma, a relationship to debasement.

Because this seems so counterintuitive, let us look at a few examples. In white capitalist, white supremacist, heteropatriarchal societies, every form of degradation causes shame. So, poor people are made to feel ashamed of themselves and their poverty, fed a daily diet of their inferiority, laziness and inadequacy. These messages that they are bombarded with are juxtaposed with the celebration of those who have wealth, mythologised as hardworking, more intelligent, superior in every way. The wealthy have easy lives of abundance. The poor battle to make ends meet and often have to do without food, electricity, water, proper healthcare or well-resourced schools. This juxtaposition and bombardment with the details of the lives of the wealthy manufactures desire for the ease enjoyed by the wealthy. This is part of the design of power. This desire seduces the poor into working harder, in search of the elusive ease, but no matter how hard they work, there are finite resources in the world.

Therefore wealth requires the hoarding of resources, which means taking away resources that would allow the poor to live decently in an equitable world. The mythology of violent power, however, casts the poor as inadequate and their inability to acquire obscene wealth as failure on their part. Repeated failure is designed to produce pain, powerlessness, defeat and ultimately shame. This is not a natural process. This is how wealth is produced and justified. In different hierarchical societies this structure is mythologised and naturalised differently, from industriousness (hard work creates wealth) to religion (hierarchy is divinely sanctioned) to biological discourses (survival and rise of the fittest) to heritage (ancestors earned privilege to be royalty).

Race and gender work in similar ways.

Part of violent gender power is in celebrating attributes associated with the masculine, and ordering the world in terms of opposites, or binaries. If masculine and feminine are opposites, and there is nothing in between, then when masculine is celebrated, feminine as its opposite has to be debased. This means that those who are marked as feminine are also debased in relation to those marked as masculine. Debasement is another way of saying made to feel inferior.

Through a similar process as for class structure in capitalist (and feudal) societies, patriarchy creates an inferiority complex in women that also depends on hatred for the feminine and therefore self-loathing. Consequently, women spend energy fixing themselves since the full human is the masculine, and given the fact that women cannot legitimately attain masculinity, the best they can do is make themselves desirable for the approval of the masculine. When this approval is perpetually deferred, more work on the self is spent. In the end, patriarchy produces a condition of women's unease in their bodies. Manifestations include the awareness of women's bodies as dirty and excessive, which then need to be disciplined, hidden, and worked on obsessively. From being told that their vaginas smell like fish, to being taught that menstrual blood and body hair are dirty (they curdle milk, they rot meat, they contaminate others), to being punished for taking up space, women are socialised to believe that there is always something wrong with us. Again, this is part of the plan. For as long as we are working on making ourselves less hairy, smelly, fleshy, and so forth, we are using energy to make ourselves smaller so that we have nothing left to fight patriarchy. It's not for nothing that the idealised feminine body in white supremacist capitalist societies is one that looks tired, and bears evidence of being worked on. Tired, hungry, distracted women are easier to control. And they are already trained to work on themselves and blame themselves for inadequacies even in the absence of sexual violence.

With race, shame is produced through slavery, colonialism and the conquest that comes from these. Enslavement, colonial onslaught and conquest lead to the breakdown of previously known patterns, rendering explanatory frameworks incapable of immediately explaining the changing world and the colonised's place in it. Reflecting on a range of slave societies, including the South African case, Gwyn Campbell and Elizabeth Elbourne introduce their collection of essays *Sex, Power and Slavery* by noting how:

> [s]lavery was accompanied by ideas of honor and dishonor. Many of the chapters in this collection, taken together, seem to suggest that across a multitude of slave societies, there were links between slavery, the control of sexuality (including a slave's lack of self-ownership and corresponding obligation to provide sexual labour), and perceptions of honor and dishonor.

Dishonour is another word for shame. Campbell and Elbourne conclude from reading across the essays in their collection, authored by different contributors analysing varied slave contexts that all of them are characterised by the allocation of honour and shame. These meanings of shame and honour are authorised – created and given power – by the control of slave sexuality. In other words, shame is induced in the slave when s/he is unable to control her/his own sexuality. The "obligation to provide sexual labour" is rape. To be a slave is to be reduced to the status of object, dehumanised and denied will and self-ownership. It is to be layered with dishonour. Under these conditions, bodily autonomy is an impossibility, inducing further shame. Slaves' bodies belonged to those who had captured or bought them. Their masters and mistresses owned their bodies, along with their productive, sexual and reproductive labour. When you are owned, chattel, consent is impossible. Rape was a core facet of enslavement.

To clarify the relationship between control of sexuality and slavocratic societies, David Brion Davis is instructive. He writes:

> [s]exual intercourse can exemplify the closest possible moment of love, merging two humans in an equal sharing of joy with an equal sharing of genes that magically gives rise to a new human life. *Yet the same physical movements can exemplify the most dehumanizing, degrading and exploitative act of conquest or warfare, including the infliction of the conqueror's genes on the enemy group.* [...] There is clearly a wide spectrum of experiences between these two extraordinary extremes. Sexual intercourse can be casual, commonplace, random, habitual, or even purchased. *But despite this variation and diversity, the relationship between a slave and a free person, especially a master, could never reach the ideal level of the first model I described, since the slave, as chattel property, could never achieve even temporary equality.* (Emphasis added)

For Davis, sexual intercourse between two consenting adults can be a range of things from love to transactional to random and everything inbetween. Sexual violence is an act of warfare that was tried and tested with success in many contexts. This is what Davis refers to. It performed on the body what guns and cannons enacted on the conquered territory. As Davis outlines, sexual control could only be violent between slaves and masters. The rape of slave women was a routine part of slave societies from the Cape to the Americas as much literature on slavery has shown. What Davis points to here is the deliberate violation and forced impregnating of slave women as part of the experience of being enslaved, a surefire way for slave masters to increase their 'property' and wealth without having to spend more money. This was not exception, but widely practised in many slave-based societies.

At her Johannesburg book launch for *Regarding Muslims: from slavery to post-apartheid,* Gabeba Baderoon noted emphatically the manner in which we will remain unable to break the stranglehold of rape in contemporary South Africa if we continue to pretend that it is a recent phenomenon. In other words, if we are at all serious about making sense of rape's hold on our society, we need to interrogate the histories of rape in South Africa. To do so, we need to look back to the kinds of work rape has done in slavocratic and colonial South Africa.

For Baderoon, it is not only important to recognise "violence and sexual exploitation" that characterised early Capetonian slaveholding society, but also that we try to take seriously the "trauma of slavery and sexual subjection" on which South Africa is founded.

The rape of slaves was an integral part of the architecture of slave-ordered Cape society. Note the place and naming of The Slave Lodge in Cape Town. Built in 1679, it served as housing for a total of approximately nine thousand slaves owned by the Dutch East India Company, prisoners and mentally ill people between 1679 and 1810. It was also known as the first brothel and "the company slave women, prostitutes. As slave status passed through the maternal line, all of the children produced by these unions were enslaved from birth, regardless of paternity", according to Mary Caroline Cravens.

The ambiguity of the housing provided by the Dutch East India Company (DEIC)/Vereenigde Oostindische Compagnie (VOC) for its slaves is illuminating. The VOC was founded in March 1602 to enable Dutch merchants to challenge the Portuguese monopoly over spice trade in Asia, as well as to better compete with British merchants. The Dutch gave the VOC rights to challenge whatever monopolies existed, while establishing its own monopoly, with free reign to colonise and enslave whoever they wished in South East Asia, to devastating effect. Having decided in 1649 to establish a refreshment station at the Cape of Good Hope, the VOC sent a group of men, led by Jan van Riebeeck. The story of the wars, enslavement and settlement by the Dutch under and after Van Riebeeck, is well known. While free people had freedom of movement, slaves did not. Consequently, unless they escaped, they were obliged to live where their owners housed them. In addition to this, given the fact that sexual coercion was part of the business of slavery, the use of The Slave Lodge as a brothel posed no contradiction within slave-ordered society. Although some historical writing suggests that the use of The Slave Lodge for this purpose preceded its use as lodging for the slaves, most records show that slaves were resident in the lodge once it was finished. This, coupled with the extremely low numbers of colonial women at the time, means that the 'prostituted' were the enslaved. Given the institutionalisation of rape in slavery at the Cape as well as in other slavocratic societies, there was no conflict between the obligational sexual labour provided by slave women as part of the lodge's function as a brothel, on the one hand, and the kind of sexual warfare and forced impregnating of slave women described by Davis earlier. Since slave women's children belonged to their owners, the institutionalised rape of slave women benefitted the DEIC/VOC.

At the same time that the rape of slave women was routine within slavery, slavocratic society created the stereotype of African hypersexuality which sought to both justify and authorise the institutionalised rape of slaves. The stereotypes held that slave women could not be raped since like all Africans they were excessively sexual and impossible to satiate. Therefore not only were slave women objects and legally incapable of being raped, they were constructed as hypersexual and therefore would not have been rapable even when free. This meant that even freed slaves could not be raped. At the same time that slave women were being routinely raped as a means to multiply their masters' slaves, slave men, especially when they were African slaves were cast as dangerously sexual, with a ravenous sexual appetite better suited to slave women, but with a particular danger to white women. Such inversion was not unique to slave society at the Cape, but was widespread not only across slave-ordered societies in the new world, but also extended into the colonial era, as I will show below.

Over the last decade, Gabeba Baderoon has produced substantial work, first for her doctoral thesis (and later book), as

43

well as in numerous articles that have painstakingly traced how the picturesque was developed to mask the persistence violence enacted on Black bodies in slavocratic society. For example, the pictures of beautiful landscapes, feminised Malay men and alluring Malay women hid the violence of slavery. Indeed, as much scholarship on empire and slavery specifically has shown, "control of sex was central to definitions of race" in colonies, as Baderoon argues in "Hidden geographies of the Cape". For Baderoon too, then, the construction of an aesthetic at the Cape was concerned with masking the layered system of violence that lay beneath.

In addition to this institutionalisation of rape within slavery, various scholars have shown how developing a language of empire also relied on an obsession with the sexual control of the colonised. This is clear in the obsessive regulation, cataloguing, drawing, pathologising and mythologising of sexuality. The language of empire, beyond slavery, was also that of a sexually violent project.

Zine Magubane's and Yvette Abrahams's scholarship is particularly instructive on how rape was retained as a core feature of colonial conquest and rule. Sexuality was an important way in which colonial Otherness was constructed, whether it be through the measuring and dissection of genitalia as Abrahams shows in her essay "The long great national insult", an extreme example of which was Sarah Baartman, or as Zine Magubane shows in her painstaking tracing of how ideas about the colonial Other evolved through the development of a pseudo medical/pseudo race-science in her book *Bringing the Empire Home*. This obsession with African genitalia and the creation of stereotypes of African excessive sexual appetites has specific effects, and reached through slavery and colonialism into the apartheid era. Traces of it can still be seen in contemporary global racisms.

Because race was made through rape and sexual difference, there was a constant preoccupation in slave-ordered societies with 'race mixing'. While the rape of slave women was profitable, it also threatened ideas of racial hierarchy and produced anxieties about race-mixing. The institutionalised rape of slave women revealed a frightening possibility (for patriarchal slave master classes) of the unspeakable sexual intercourse between white women and slave men. This anxiety was about the loss of control over the bodies of white women, as much as it was about the idea of white women becoming unpure.

Anxiety over miscegenation – that horrid word for people procreating across race – is really an anxiety about rape. Sorcha Gunne and Zoë Brigley Thompson remind us that:

> [i]n thinking about rape, colonialism and the construction of community or a national identity, it is useful to note that in patriarchal society racial purity and sexual purity are not mutually exclusive. As the female body is the locus for reproduction, it becomes a site of immense concern to the male patriarch.

It is the fear of the white woman's body producing what the slave woman produces that creates the patriarchal anxiety about miscegenation, since the slave master is directly implicated in the project of violently impregnating slave women and producing the very 'miscegenation' that he fears in his own house. Rape is such a core tenet of colonial rule that Gunne and Thompson also list examples of Spanish colonial armies celebrating conquest by raping and abducting colonised Native American women, such as was the case in Mexico.

This is because, as historian Yvette Abrahams shows, dispossession has been a history of how rape, slavery and colonialism worked in entangled and mutually reinforcing ways. In "Was Eva raped?" Abrahams insists:

> [i]n reconsidering the process whereby the Khoisan came to lose, not only their land, but also much of their culture and history, it seemed to me that slavery and rape were two crucial explanatory mechanisms.

Whereas in many other places where slavery has left its ugly imprint, we have an archive of slave narratives, in the South African case, the lives of slaves come to us through snippets in court records, diaries, colonial journals and letters. Because raping slave women was both widespread and not a crime, colonial record offers a challenge of evidence. Abrahams and Patricia Scully write of an incident where a man convicted of raping a woman had the sentence reversed when the judge realised that the woman had not in fact been a white woman. We can deduce from similarities with slavery elsewhere, including from the diaries and notes of abolitionists like Thomas Pringle who lived in South Africa and directly debunked claims by Caribbean and South African slave owners that slavery in these two places was milder than the most brutal instances in North America. We can also deduce much from deliberate coincidences like The Slave Lodge being a brothel, as well as population numbers. We can also engage in informed and considered speculative historical enquiry, as Abrahams suggests. She writes:

> How do you study a crime through sources which were assuredly not written by the victims and could have been written by the perpetrator? It is possible to theoretically deduce the occurrence of rape in general, but how do you prove the existence of a specific rape? It is hard enough today, in court cases where the victim and the perpetrator are still alive. The problems of studying rape in previous centuries seemed insuperable. The studies I have used approach the subject through court records. However this method is limited to cases where a charge was actually brought to court, an unlikely event in a case of rape by a slave woman, or *inboekseling* woman, against a master. *Slaves were objects to be used and as such could neither consent or dissent to the manner of their use. In a legal sense they could not be raped. Thus the rapes of slave women were unlikely to appear in court records.* Scully's chapter on rape in a post-emancipation context shows that during some thirty years only one case of rape of a Black woman against a white man was ever brought, and this was dropped before it came to court. If this was the case in the mid-nineteenth century, it must have been even more difficult for earlier periods. (Emphasis mine)

While it would benefit us to be able to speak about specific slave women by name in the same way that I sometimes do in discussions in the other chapters in this book, and as we are able to do as scholars of slave narratives when we have autobiographical narratives, the South African case presents challenges. For the purposes of this book, it will have to suffice to trace the threads and interpret what is available, to follow the evidence and read it against what else we know about slavocratic societies.

If the sources are unreliable, do we then just fold our hands and give up? In my essay "Like three tongues in one mouth", I argue that it is, in fact, possible to learn various things about women who did not leave a written record and who are largely filtered to us through records written by those who did not see them as human at all, saw them as partly human or who were shaped by colonial ways of seeing the world. Abrahams argues similarly, by showing how many aspects of Eva/Krotoa's life as she comes through to us – rendered sometimes as inexplicable – can be made sense of when we know some of the manifestations of Rape Trauma Syndrome (RTS).

Researching a later epoch and a different region of South Africa, Robert Edgerton has shown the extensive use of rape as a weapon of warfare by the British as they advanced into various parts of what is now the Eastern Cape. In his book *Africa's armies: from honor to infamy*, Edgerton writes of how British and Boer numbers motivated them to advance into Xhosa territory in the 1790s, an assault that was met and resisted by Xhosa warriors in the hundred-year war that has been dubbed the 'eight frontier wars' in colonial lexicon. I want to quote him at length here to demonstrate various aspects of the relationship between colonialism and rape, and I do so also attentive to what is problematic about lenses applied to interpret the specific moments and sequence narrated:

In the 1830s wide-ranging British patrols ravaged Xhosaland, burning houses and crops and stealing cattle, driving the Xhosa farther north and filling them with despair. *In response to British depredations that sometimes included rape and murder*, the Xhosa bought firearms and powder and made ready for war. In 1834 another fifteen thousand men marched south burning farms, making off with cattle, and killing white settlers. Even the brash and pompous commander, Sir Harry Smith, came to respect the Xhosa fighters as 'bold, intrepid and skillful.' The fighting eventually calmed because the Xhosa chose to return north to care for the thousands of cattle they had stolen. More 'frontier' wars followed during years of guerilla combat in which the Xhosa excelled. Despite their success in this kind of fighting, at which the red coated British were at a great disadvantage, the Xhosa nevertheless sometimes chose to attack fortified British positions. In the early 1850s, they attacked a British fort for over five hours before withdrawing with heavy losses. While their judgement in making such an attack can be questioned, their valor was never in doubt. *Despite the escalating brutality of the British troops and white volunteers who often killed Xhosa children, throughout the entire century of warfare, the Xhosa were known to have killed only one white woman – perhaps by mistake – and they never killed any white children.* (Emphasis mine)

Today we almost take it for granted that rape is an inevitable part and consequence of war. Part of what this passage reveals, and indeed many other instances in Edgerton's book from different African colonial contexts, is the way in which the connection between rape and war is not automatic. It comes from a very specific idiom, from the colonial archive. It is a deliberate investment in using sexual violence as part of conquest, not an accidental one. Because the Xhosa warriors come from a different logic of war, they avoid attacks and retaliation routes that might catch women and children in the cross-fire. This determination sees a frustrated Edgerton earlier in the text wishing the warriors had attacked at night when they had an advantage.

After poring over colonial writings from fiction to journals and letters from different parts of the colonised world, Ania Loomba writes of the manner in which consistently in the European colonial imagination, the coloniser was represented as rapist and the 'discovered/conquered' land as the naked woman. Here, we see that the Empire imagines itself as rapist of land and people. Therefore the centrality of rape as a weapon of colonial war is not an accident. Rather, rape occupies pride of place in the colonial artillery. Loomba continues:

[w]e have seen how the spectrum of representations encode the rape and plunder of colonised countries by figuring the latter as naked women and figuring the colonisers as masters/rapists. But the threat of native rebellion produces a very different kind of colonial stereotype which presents the colonised as a (usually dark-skinned) rapist who comes to ravish the white woman who in turn comes to symbolise European culture. This stereotype reverses the trope of colonialism-as-rape, and thus, it can be argued, deflects the violence of the colonial encounter from the coloniser to the colonised. Understood variously as either a native reaction to imperial rape, or as a pathology of the darker races, or even as a European effort to rationalise colonial guilt, the figure of the 'black' rapist is commonplace enough to be seen as a necessary/ permanent feature of the colonial landscape.

Loomba then proceeds to discuss a wealth of scholarship that shows that the figure of the Black rapist takes on a particular visibility across various colonial contexts, especially in times of great anxiety about 'native resistance', and that this is especially the case when there is no record of actual rape by South Asians or Africans. Thus the colonial inversion is explained in Loomba's passage above where she shows that European colonial literature wrote about colonisers as celebrated rapists of land and women from the conquered land, whether Africa, Asia or the Americas. This literature is rife, and the earlier example of the Spanish colonists' celebration by raping Native American women is also part of this motif. At the same time, the colonial imagination constructed the 'Hindoo rapist' or 'slave rapist' or other 'native rapist' as a stereotype to manage colonial anxiety. Part of what this

49

reveals is how deeply enmeshed rape and warfare were in colonial imaginaries because even resistance to colonial rule has to be thought of in these terms, even if evidence suggests that rebellions take different forms and not the rape of white women. In all senses, then, it is clear that the stereotype of the unrapable Black woman, along with that of the rapist Black man reveals more about the colonial unconscious and predetermined ideas than what is likely to happen given patterns of resistance against colonial rule.

If the register of rape was introduced by slavery and entrenched by colonial conquest, it had certainly taken hold by the time apartheid was introduced. Rape had become entrenched, and various other forms of violence assisted in strengthening its foothold. Jacklyn Cock notes that in the South African Defence Force (SADF), "the core of military training is to inculcate aggression and equate it with masculinity … that the army cultivates a form of masculinity that involves insensitivity, aggressiveness, competitiveness, violence and the censure of emotional expression." The business of war had by now become associated primarily – and sometimes exclusively – with the militarised project of masculinity that Cock describes.

Writing about the decade from 1983–1992, Jenni Irish insists that part of understanding the extreme violence of the era – 14 000 deaths, half of which were in Natal alone – is taking into account the various ways in which such political violence was gendered.

What I have traced is the manner in which political violence was always gendered. It is therefore unsurprising to read Irish's findings on the gendered nature of political violence in the eighties.

The sexual violence Irish writes about may not be exclusively from white male colonists, but its targets are still largely Black women. It is violence that takes for granted women's vulnerabilities, such as the likelihood of being alone with children and the elderly in the home, unarmed and unable to flee speedily during massacres, as well as their inability to secure safety even once they arrive in refugee shelters. This is because:

> [v]ery often people are packed into venues and forced to sleep on the ground with possibly one blanket. The women have no

privacy and often become targets for sexual abuse and assault. In one refugee camp on the South coast at least three women were forced to flee the camp after being raped by men in the camp. Confidential discussion with other women in the camp revealed a chain of sexual harassment. Most women however, are scared to report these goings on and some choose to leave the camp and sleep in the bushes rather than put up with continued harassment.

In a context where reporting rape also requires entering an additional layer of vulnerability and unpredictability, women who have been displaced by political violence, survived massacres, and have no place to return to were, therefore, in a particularly precarious position. Many other comparative contexts have also shown that when there is upheaval, conflict and militarisation, rapes, in particular, increase. But when women report being raped by policemen as well, the likelihood of reporting and accessing justice retreats even further.

Jenni Irish writes that:

[i]n at least ten cases brought to the Human Rights Commission, women in the Durban area complained of being raped by one notorious policeman. One social worker dealing with some of these cases alleged that the man in question had raped the women and from that point on, the women would be his girlfriends and he 'would call on them when required.' The women were told that should they attempt to refuse to 'co-operate' with him, their families' lives would be endangered. In the above cases, the women were faced with the option of continued rape or the possible loss of family members. To make matters worse, those that were forced to 'accept' these terms were then isolated by other members of the community and peers because they were perceived to be the 'girlfriends' of a notorious killer.

The above uncovers the conditions of precarity as agents of violent power continue to brutalise women, placing them in even more dangerous positions open to secondary victimisation and shame, unable to access help, justice and healing.

In her essay "Rape in South Africa: an invisible part of apartheid's legacy", Sue Armstrong writes:

> [i]n situations of conflict, rape as a means of asserting male power over women tends to increase in incidence and intensity .... This has certainly been the case in South Africa, where the incidence of rape and other forms of gender violence, has soared.

She further notes until the abolishment of the death penalty, no white man had been hanged for rape, whereas the only Black men who were hung for rape had been convicted of raping white women; no white man or Black man had been convicted and sentenced to death for raping a Black woman.

By the time apartheid is in decline, the rape of Black women is so entrenched that it is extensively practised beyond the ranks of state agents. Armstrong, quoting Heather Reganass from the National Institute for Crime Prevention and Rehabilitation of Offenders, continues:

> [w]hen we started investigating, we discovered that rape, particularly of black women, was so prolific in South Africa that it was just accepted by everybody: social workers, doctors, policemen, and even the victim herself. A black woman's life was considered valueless, and what had happened to her unimportant. We wanted to question that assumption: rape is abhorrent and cannot be condoned, whoever the victim is.

Rape of Black women, as I have shown, was central to slavery, colonialism and it is, as Sue Armstrong points out, a legacy of the past that stretched into the present, beyond the boundaries of apartheid. I have not included examples here of women raped or threatened with rape in detention, although this was not uncommon.

It has been my aim in this chapter to trace the development of rape as a weapon against women that is both widespread and not taken seriously. What this chapter has uncovered is how rape became such a powerful language with which to control women in South Africa, and the scale of it, and as the last few examples show, it is a language that is now an established part of South African power. Yet, with all of this history, Desireé Hansson cautions that in a context where:

> both theory and research suggest that black women who are raped by white men, and rape survivors who do not fulfill the stereotypical male definition of femininity are discriminated against within the legal system, it is vital that the impact of recent rape reforms on differentially oppressed women be evaluated carefully.

Perhaps this should not be surprising given the fact that the criminal justice system is based on Roman Dutch Law, the same law that once rendered Black women unrapable, in a phenomenon Jane Bennett calls "metaphorical deafness" in her essay "Enough lip service". She defines metaphorical deafness as "a strategy of colonial and patriarchal approaches to gender" that refuses to engage with concrete realities "in which gendered dynamics play a fast and furious role".

Like Bennett, I suspect that the way out of these histories "demands reorientation, unfamiliar relations to power, and seemingly irreconcilable choices". Black women are the most likely to be raped because of these combined histories about who matters least, not because of specific essences of Black men; it still bears noting that across categories of men, not just white colonist men, rapists rape the women longest burdened with assumptions of unrapability. Still, all women are in danger of rape.

CHAPTER 3

Ruling violence

Twenty-one years ago, South Africa had its first democratic election, and as a country that is particularly fond of milestones, we reminded ourselves repeatedly of the significance of 27 April 1994. The twenty-first year of South Africa's democracy also presents an opportunity to reflect on the many ways in which the country we live in differs from the one we left behind. It also offers metaphoric maturity to reflect on the failures, limitations and disappointments we have gone through, as it becomes clearer that many aspects of our democracy need to be revisited if we are to move forward to a country we all want to live in.

Twenty-one years on, violence continues to retain a strong grip on our lives that postpones the attainment of the kind of free society we so optimistically awaited in 1994. The saturation of our lives with violence is a legacy of unfinished pasts and it is also evidence of emboldening forms of violence enabled in post-apartheid South Africa. It is no longer enough to say that this is better than apartheid; almost anything is better than apartheid. Loosening the stranglehold on violence is going to require fewer excuses and more imagination.

In 2015 the cracks are clear: there have been two explosions of violence against Africans and South Asians who are assumed not to hold legitimate South African passports. Both these events have shaken us to the core as a society, even as we continue to disagree passionately about what they reveal about us. Should we call such attacks xenophobia? And if we do, what do they illustrate about our relationships to ourselves, Blackness, the continent and the value of human life in South Africa? We will probably not agree any time soon about what all of these explosions of violence against those deemed 'foreigners' mean. I know that as I continue to write about the spectacle of burning, broken bodies of those safe to violate, we are seeing the retention of gendered, classed and raced violence that is connected to many other patterns of belonging and interaction in South Africa that we view as normal. It is easy to see the young men who attack and kill 'foreigners' in the street as pathological, to pretend if we say they are criminals, their actions are not also political. In fact, the behaviour of the economically marginal young men has everything to do with all of us, regardless of how we live. Their behaviour is not out of step with the high levels of gendered violence from rape to sexual harassment to intimate femicide. It is also not separate from the orientation of South African capital to the rest of the continent and the world. I have developed both of these arguments of how 'typically South African' this negrophobic violence is in my writing elsewhere, and will therefore not do so here.

In the twenty-first year of our democracy we have also survived the Marikana tragedy and continue to await the release of the report of another moment of deep collective trauma as miners were shot down. In a sequence of events played out to increasingly disbelieving audiences, the shootings at Marikana were punctuated by explanations that created more mystification than clarity. Rehad Desai's brilliant film *Miners Shot Down* bravely cuts through the smoke and mirrors. President Zuma's June 2015 release of the Farlam Commission on Marikana report, three months after he received it, did little to assuage the public disillusionment with lack of accountability. This is especially so, given the exoneration of all political figures, and the apportioning of blame for all deaths from the Marikana massacre to the striking miners.

As we approach the fortieth anniversary of the June 16 student uprisings, radical student movements like #RhodesMustFall show the failure of previous projects to transform South Africa's universities. This is all also happening against the backdrop of a crumbling public education system. The young people of the #RhodesMustFall movement, along with their comrades in allied movements are impatient with not just the slow pace of transformation at universities, but also the continuing violence against Black people in these spaces. The romance of a new country is gone, and the children that should have inherited Mandela's dream continue to live under the brutalisation of raced, gendered terror. Their strategies and rage are not entirely different from the energy, anger and hope that we associate with the Soweto 1976 student uprising. As we celebrate, commemorate and reflect on milestones along our liberation timeline, Soweto 1976 reminds us of how actively contested education and language once were, and how important it is not to take activities in those spheres for granted. When the Black staff at the University of Cape Town who organise under #TransformUCT insist on curriculum change, they also drive home the failure of the transformation agenda and the urgency of unapologetically decolonising universities. These are strong statements against institutional violence, often met with criminalisation and violence that should not be the norm twenty-one years after 1994.

We are also eighteen months away from the sixtieth anniversary of the Women's March on the Union Buildings protesting the extension of passes to black women. Ten years ago, I was privy to the words of one of the march's leaders, Ms Sophia Williams de Bruyn, as she addressed various audiences, which included the Council for Scientific and Industrial Research's (CSIR) Women's Day Breakfast in Tshwane on 8 August, an address before the Lilian Ngoyi Memorial Lecture at the University of South Africa on 25 August, and her address at the Commemorative March of the fiftieth anniversary of the Women's March on 9 August. With her, we reflected on how tall South African women stand in history, and on the reality that defiance was no stranger to them, so that at a time when there were no cellular phones and moving up and down the country was heavily policed, 20 000 women made it to the planned women's march. As Ms Williams de Bruyn, then deputy speaker of the Gauteng Legislature, reminded us, many were sidetracked, detained and barred from attending in various ways. Had this not been so, we would have known more accurately how many women left their homes for that herstoric March.

Given this example of women's political organisation, it is particularly troubling to reflect on the epidemic of violence against women – rape, femicide, public attacks and stripping, routine sexual harassment, women like Nandi Mbizane who disappear from their homes without a trace, or like Constable Rasuge who get murdered by intimate partners and whose remains are discovered many years later, women like Khwezi once exiled for laying a charge of rape against a powerful man who subsequently rose to the nation's highest office, the decreasing reports of rape to the police which suggest decreasing confidence in the possibility of justice for rape survivors. It is almost a decade since the Jacob Zuma rape trial. This is what One in Nine activists were reminding those who participated in the celebratory march by the ANC Women's League in August 2012. Carrying a banner with the words "No cause for celebration", and staging a die-in that crossed the path of the ANCWL marchers, these feminist activists were reminding the marchers – many of them powerful women in government and in the majority party – of the huge gap between the country's gender legislation and women's experiences of living under siege from gendered violence.

In 2006, we were also invited to cast our minds' eyes to the anniversary of the 1906 Bhambatha rebellion/uprising against enforced colonial poll tax, to ponder what it means to be closing our second decade since the first Truth and Reconciliation Commission (TRC) hearings in East London in 1996, and celebrating almost twenty years of our Constitution, a founding document that allowed us to project an image of our society as it would be if we were our best selves. In this way, the Constitution is an aspirational document, to borrow Homi Bhabha's 2002 phrase, just like Bishop Tutu's naming of us as 'the rainbow people of God' was aspirational. This labelling of South Africans as the rainbow nation, similar to the provisions of the Constitution, would bring us closer to the society described in both. The labels were aspirational because they gave hope, a hope that sometimes feels like it is in danger of permanently slipping away. The Constitution as a project describes how we should relate to one another, what we should be able to assume and invest in one another, what embracing and accepting that we are all entitled to freedom really means. So, it does not hold the thoughts, ideologies, values or held morals of the majority of South Africans.

It is aspirational because it defines us generously as our best selves, in ways that dramatically move away from the manifold forms of legislated and institutionalised oppression under the 'chaotic nightmare' that became apartheid, as Achille Mbembe might say. The Constitution positions us as freedom-loving and just people who would have freedom enjoyed by all. As one of the late Nadine Gordimer's characters in her 1998 novel *The House Gun* says, it is a document of what should be a 'collective morality of a people'.

It is fitting that all these anniversaries coincide with the second decade of the writing of the Constitution, because this allows us to reflect upon the ways in which we think about our past and future. Let me explain. When national anniversaries come to us in isolation, by which I mean one per year rather than the cluster South Africans were presented with in 2006, and as we will be in 2016, we can well be forgiven for playing up the peculiarity, or 'specialness', of that particular event and airbrushing the larger context out. So, twelve years ago, as we celebrated ten years since our first democratic election, we arguably had never been more vocal about how far we had come. We were self-congratulatory and perhaps re-lived how free we felt when we cast that first vote in April 1994 as well as the euphoria we felt for the remainder of that year. We enjoyed the fact that none of the naysayers and prophets of doom had been right about the fate of our country post-freedom.

Young artists working in all genres seemed to intensify the production of a South African aesthetic: cheeky and unapologetically mixed as it drew inspiration from wherever it saw fit, and so it became 'Afro-chic', more kwaito, more 'Afro-pop', more Mzantsi, and so on. Focusing on such a beautiful moment from our past, and how well we had taken to the new hard-won freedoms, it makes sense that we had a year-long party, as we should have had. At the same time, that is the beauty of having only one anniversary in a year.

The year 2006 was different, and the multiple anniversaries did not just mean that we were much busier. This coincidence of multiple historical markings in 2006 meant that our feelings and thoughts from the various anniversaries overlapped. We thought about 16 June in relation to present legal language protections, the tensions around mother-tongue instruction and the school system, and now a decade later the uprisings at university campuses. We could not divorce the student uprisings from the drawing up of the Constitution and/or from the TRC, the Women's March, the Bhambatha rebellion and/or from the assassination of Mozambican president Samora Machel and his colleagues. A year such as this reminded us of how much has been fought for over centuries in order for us to enjoy the freedoms we have: how many people have fled, bled, sacrificed and also how many others have rebelled, fought and planned. The year 2006 drove home that much still needs to be fought for: that as brilliantly spectacular as our 1994 and 2004 were, many freedoms still need to be attained and defended. It became apparent then, as we allowed various formative historical moments to rub against one another, encircle one another and overlap, that our history could not be a timeline, and that the continuities shifted and returned to us with new implications.

The most striking thread that links all these events is fighting and the presence of violence. The Bhambatha and June 1976 uprisings pitched defiance, self-assertion and brutal violence against each other. On the one hand, there were people refusing to be subjected to increasing legal and institutionalised oppression, on the other, was a local colonial and then, later, apartheid state machinery that responded with brute force. The Bhambatha warriors defended themselves against colonial brutality, and so, as is true in many anti-colonial conflicts, violence became both the onslaught and self-defence. The TRC offered us another chance to look at the ways in which violence permeated otherwise very different aspects of South African society, by opening up our long historical consciousness, our 'long memoried' collective self, as Guyanese poet Grace Nichols might say.

Slavery and colonialism were rooted in violence and violation, in the negation of some lives and tearing apart of families, and the ingraining of self-hate. Self-defence in the face of colonisation also found expression as taking up arms, leading to centuries of warfare across the breadth of the African continent, and later the entire African world we call the diaspora today.

Building on this, apartheid capitalised on the physical violence of contestation through the militaristic control as well as the structural violence of the economy. Systematically brutalising Black people through various forms of impoverishment, displacement, disenfranchisement and military occupation, apartheid also ensured that white South Africans were heavily armed through the enforced conscription that helped prop up apartheid South Africa, and maintain a low-level war between the state and comrades.

Given the patriarchal structure of both Black and white societies in South Africa, this high militarisation could only take on gendered forms and play itself out along sharply gendered lines. Children were socialised into societies that were constituted by violent interaction in their very fabric. Even the playground was not free from the scourge of violence and militarism, as was evidenced by popular Boy Scout and Girl Guide troops in Black communities or *veld en vlei* holidays in teenage Afrikaner settings.

The failure to dismantle what Jacklyn Cock calls 'the ideology of militarism' in a new South Africa is directly implicated in what ails post-apartheid South Africa. And it is this silence around the connections between accepting the ever-presence of violence as a given, on the one hand, and the absence of discussions around how it affects us as a society, on the other, which continues to trouble. In other words, when we take violence as a constant companion in our midst – but one that we pretend is invisible – we can only continue to live in a messy state.

This 'ideology of militarism' requires the same kind of rigour to dismantle as other forms of control, so silence and denial are not a way out. Given its pervasiveness, it finds expression in the academic, business and non-governmental sectors, in culture, language and entertainment and government institutions. It is often hidden under the epithet of 'discipline' in the broad left when refusal to adhere to certain precepts is often seen as the absence of discipline. One of the problems with this concept of discipline, which seeks to repress interiority in favour of outwardly visible manifestations of order, is that it also helps to mask other repressive systems that work to support the ideology of militarism.

The TRC offered us various windows into how violence and silence work through the ambit of discipline. Much has been written about what was said, sayable and difficult to articulate at the TRC. Thenjiwe Mtintso has commented on the difficulty of speaking about the sexual abuse women activists suffered at the hands of the state and some of their male comrades. At the same time, she has criticised how silence also protected women who acted on behalf of the apartheid state and violated the human rights of others. However, as Nthabiseng Motsemme's stellar and groundbreaking work on women's testimonies and women's voices at the TRC has shown, "the mute always speak", so that the effects of silence and silencing are not always the wishing away of what cannot be spoken.

Today, we have a Constitution that affirms women's dignity and rights to full humanity; at the same time, there are silences and gaps on the gendered dimensions of our past. These silences are directly implicated in the siege under which we live, in the continued dominance of violence across different areas of South African life. This situation is sometimes referred to as the 'puzzling' South African contradiction and, when so labelled, it is often by those who claim to find this situation impossible to explain, or account for.

Perhaps a better way to arrive at the core of this 'mystery', this 'South African contradiction', requires that we explore what it is South Africans have spoken about, and continue to discuss publicly.

The anti-apartheid struggle was articulated in the broad strokes that would lead us to a country free of all oppressions and discrimination based on race, class, gender, sexual orientation, religion, language, geographical location and ability. This is the country of the Constitution. From slave resistance, anti-colonial resistance to the Unity Movement, African National Congress, Pan Africanist Congress, Black Consciousness Movement, the South African Communist Party, and those aligned with these movements, freedom from apartheid was seen as synonymous with freedom from the burden of race, from racist oppression and persecution. Yet the legacy of apartheid continues to be felt by the vast majority of the Black poor, who are written out of capital and most victimised. It also continues to be felt by Black South Africans whose growing impatience with untransformed institutions is becoming increasingly audible in 2015. Although now free from state racism, they feel the effects of a mutating, oppressive, capitalist system in their workplaces, for those who have such jobs. For the more affluent, race and class still exert control either in the backlash against affirmative action, tokenism, the demonisation of Black Economic Empowerment, untransformed institutions in which white supremacy is again becoming emboldened, or the pressure to participate and be absorbed into a culture of rampant materialism and consumerism.

These are problems that continue to haunt us. All of these processes are gendered, although you might not think so from the bulk of national public discourse. There are concerted efforts to address disparities of race and class. These focus on social transformation and are mindful of the oft-repeated warning about ensuring that we had both political and economic freedom in a South African democracy. It is important that we continue to ask questions about how this is translated, who is locked out, and how ideas about societal transformation are being narrowed down.

The discourses of gender in the South African public sphere are very conservative in the main: they speak of 'women's empowerment' in ways that are not transformative, and as a consequence, they exist very comfortably alongside overwhelming evidence that South African women are not empowered: the rape and other gender-based violence statistics, the rampant sexual harassment at work and public spaces, the overloaded maintenance and family courts, the siege on Black lesbians and raging homophobia, the very public and relentless circulation of misogynist imagery, metaphors and language.

When I first offered the bulk of these reflections, I did so as part of the 2006 Ruth First Memorial Lecture, and I wondered out loud, what Ruth First, communist, anti-racist, journalist, historian, among many others things, would make of the South Africa she fought for. Asking this question again in 2015 is even more disturbing. I realise that with all the anger, disappointment and criticism, I was still much more optimistic in 2006 than I am as I update this essay. What kind of critique might First have come up with? We know that she did not shy away from difficult questions even within the left. I think she would have found contemporary South African 'gender talk' in need of much critique.

This talk of 'the empowerment of women', as currently employed and aired in South Africa, rests on the assumption that ensuring that some women have access to wealth, positions in government and corporate office, is enough gender-progressive work for our society. This assumption is flawed on various levels, even if increased representation of women across all sectors of our society is a worthwhile and necessary project.

Firstly, not all women have access to high office because class, homophobia, race and xenophobia mediate women's access to power. At its best, therefore, this formula would empower a small select number of women in the terrain of work, and leave the rest 'unempowered'. Secondly, the dominant talk of 'empowerment of women' also translates into the expectation that women should adapt to the current system, being 'empowered' into position, rather than transforming the formal workplace into a space that is more receptive to women's contributions, needs and wants. It requires that women in this country try to attain, within the formal workplace, the status of 'honorary men' as Mamphela Ramphele has said of another time, a concept she expanded on in a 1998 interview with Kimberley Yates and myself, as well as in her essay "Political widowhood in South Africa: the embodiment of ambiguity". Thus, although women's representation in all sectors of our society initially emerged as a radical and feminist call for transformation in the interest of a more equitable society, the version we have now, at least in public talk, is so watered down that it threatens to stall social transformation. It also means that those attempts, successful and failed, by women to alter the economic landscape are routinely under-reported and undervalued. It is against this invisibilisation of women's real transformative work that one of the most powerful women in South Africa's business sector, Nolitha Fakude, spoke when she told the South African National Editors' Forum (SANEF) gathering that 'you do us no favours when you make us seem like no more than pretty faces' in reporting on major Black Economic Empowerment deals.

The hijacked 'women's empowerment' talk is also flawed in a linked, third, sense. As Shireen Hassim reminds us, "changing inequities in social and economic power will require not just the increased representation of women within the state, but also the increased and assertive representation of poor women within the state, as well as a strong feminist movement outside the state." In other words, it is only through a comprehensive contestation of representation and voice across class that meaningful gender transformation is possible.

The fourth flaw emerges when we recognise that this conservative 'women's empowerment' debate only really applies to women while they are in the official 'public space': in the workplace. A completely different set of rules, framed in direct contradiction to the ostensible 'women's empowerment' discourse continues to govern the 'private' world of the home, and other spaces in between: public transport, the streets, clubs, restaurants, shebeens, etc.

Outside of work, the dominant gender-talk is that women must adhere to very limiting notions of femininity. The recycling of the 'cult of femininity' takes place across sectors, as public culture demonstrates. Indeed, it is so pervasive that it retains high visibility among the ranks of ostensibly 'highly empowered' women. In interview after media interview, the question is posed to economically powerful women, "Who are you really?" Thus, pressure is applied to prove that they exhibit traditionally feminine traits, in other words, that as powerful as such women are at work, they submit to the patriarchal 'cult of femininity' elsewhere, illustrating that South African media are as much a product of this society as they are of a global late-capitalist patriarchal order.

As I argued in my book, *A Renegade called Simphiwe*, the discourse of women's empowerment also serves to strengthen the idea of The New South African Woman in ways that both idealise her and set her up as in constant danger of falling from grace and becoming a train wreck.

This highly circulated 'cult of femininity' is not unconnected to the experiences of many women. The Republic of South Africa, therefore, has the contradictory situation where women are legislatively empowered, and yet we do not feel safe in our streets or homes. Truly empowered women do not live with the haunting fear of rape, sexual harassment, smash-and-grabs and other violent intrusions into their spaces, bodies and psyches. A country that empowers women would grant us our entitlement of freedom of movement, sexual autonomy, bodily integrity and safety. A genuinely gender-progressive country is without the gender-based violence statistics that South Africa has, making South African women collectively a majority (at 52 per cent) under siege. There simply are no two-ways about it. It certainly does not watch and participate in 'curative'/'corrective' rapes against its most marginal: Black lesbians and/or poor women.

The current hijacked 'women's empowerment' hype is not a real conversation because it is not transformative. It is a smokescreen, and assumes that women are the only ones who need empowerment, as limited as routes to such empowerment are. It leaves the 'cult of femininity' intact and violent masculinities untouched.

Gender-transformative work requires that masculinities – Black, white, straight, queer – be radically revisited and transformed in the interest of a country that is not just gender-equitable on paper. It demands honesty in dealing with the siege under which all South African women continue to live. Thenjiwe Mtintso once remarked, "You find there are comrades who bow to the question of gender equality but in terms of their own behaviour are quite different", whereas Roshila Nair (2001) wrote a poem about the same contradiction:

> let's say it loud
> about the other day
> how we were talking
> about that Comrade X
> who went home
> and gave his wife
> a blue eye,
> after we'd all clapped
> an hour before
> for the liberation
> speech he gave
> with such conviction

We are not speaking these truths enough, and until we are able to address them as well as the long histories we come from, approach them with imaginative new ways to break the patterns, we will continue to live with the scourge of gender-based violence. And it does not help to pretend, as millions do, that our denial will protect us. It has not done so, thus far. The grip of violence is tightening around our collective necks. Those who pretend to be stunned by the statistics are lazily not making the connections between the various ways in which what is 'normal' heterosexual 'play' contain codes that inscribe feminine passivity and masculine aggression.

We saw it in the twist of the arm as teenage girls, the assumption that girls 'play hard to get' and therefore should be pursued at all costs regardless of what they say, the bizarre and oppressive claims that women cannot say what they mean and mean what they say.

Consequently, a man can see that an out lesbian is aroused and decide to have 'sex' with her since an aroused woman cannot be left alone. We have to eliminate the equally ridiculous claims that as women, we are so stupid, so passive and beaten down that we can only wear short skirts, revealing or tight clothes, get drunk, wear kangas, smoke cigarettes or do drugs, do anything to signal to men that we are aroused and are asking for it. It is a strange country we live in where women are so ostensibly empowered and yet cannot communicate what they want sexually. It is also a very strange country where women need to be 'cured' of being lesbians since this is made out to be just another way in which we play hard to get and put ourselves out of the ownership of violent men.

It is a ridiculous lie, and it is not new. We know what is responsible for the scourge of gender-based violence, and we need to confront violent masculinities. We need to confront and reject violent men and the patriarchal men and women who protect and enable them. Audre Lorde said, again and again, "Your silence will not protect you." Our silence, says bell hooks, is complicity.

There is no fence-sitting on this one, no convenient grey areas.

Nadine Hutton, as she then was, had an exhibition as part of the 2006 Ruth First Lecture when I first presented this essay. In that work, her camera points to some of these patterns of violent masculinity and the cyclical nature of violence. Her work also painfully indicts South African society because although the subject – the woman – whose story she documents is a white working-class woman, her story is in many ways not spectacular. By that I do not mean that she is not important or unique as an individual human being, but rather that the pattern of abuse is played out in many homes across this country across province, race and class.

Gender-based violence is very ordinary: it is everywhere, commonplace, made to seem normal. Marianne Thamm highlights some of this when she speaks about the routine sexual harassment of girls in her middle-class white suburb as she grew up, when she zooms in on "three men, all of them from 'good backgrounds' and fathers of children who were my friends, they tried to cop a feel when no one was looking ... I can still feel the clammy grip of their hands on my elbow or arm."

From experiences lived, shared and related, we know how widespread – endemic – gender-based violence is. We can undo it only by unmasking the collective denial, that lie that we tell about how we do not know who is abusing and raping up and down the length of South Africa. We do know who the man who slaps his girlfriend around at a party is, or the one who drags her across the parking lot, the teacher who impregnates school girls with our permission because we do not hold him accountable for statutory rape, the taxi driver who tells homophobic and misogynist jokes, the 'comrade' who assumes that he can touch whichever woman he finds attractive, the 'leader' who harasses women in his organisation, and the colleague who rapes. We know who these men are, and when we say nothing, we are complicit with how they spread gender-based violence with our protection. When we are the kind of women who never believe a girl or another woman's narrative of rape, or believe her but tell her to keep quiet anyway because her story will embarrass him and/or us, we are complicit with the siege under which we live.

We need to rethink our own behaviour and responses to gender-based violence if we are these kinds of women, and we need to be able to disown women of all classes who defend violent men, and who protect them, not just the ostensibly poor who will perform outside a court room.

At the same time, while it is not just men who are responsible for the scourge under which we live, since many women think that patriarchy rewards its foot soldiers, every man in this country has a responsibility to counter gender-based violence and enable meaningful gender-transformation. All men need to show up and reject the silence that protects violent masculinities. They need to think about how they speak to and about women and girls. They need to question what they were taught and what they are teaching boys and younger men when they conflate strength with being emotionally hard and excusing violence, when they think women are just bodies and that we need to be controlled.

One of my favourite television shows in 2006 offered us a vision of a young, highly intelligent, creatively inspired Black man who, episode after episode, season after season, brought issues of women's sexual autonomy, bodily integrity, gender-based violence, progressive masculinities and breaking patterns of violent masculinity into our living rooms. And yet this is one of the most popular and watched programmes and he is a top entertainment personality in South Africa.

Now I am not holding Bonginkosi Dlamini up as a god, and he certainly is not paying me to say this. Subsequent to this public lecture and first publication of excerpts from it, Dlamini's relationships with men, women and violence received extensive media attention with conflictual reports. It is therefore important to highlight this, as I revise this essay for publication. The point I was making was about the existence of a specific show, whose challenging of gender power was exciting, not an endorsement of how Dlamini may live his life. That show illustrated quite clearly that there is another way, and there is a space within contemporary South Africa for 'freed zones' on gender, and there are people receptive to this message.

I am borrowing the concept of liberated zones from the FRELIMO talk in the Mozambican guerrilla movement; I think that the histories of freed zones that we have as legacy in this region should inspire us. The point of freed zones, of course, is that ultimately they spread so that the whole country is one large liberated zone.

Yes, it is hard work.

It is very hard work, but we have embraced the need to do hard work before. Revolutionary work is always hard work, as Steve Biko also taught us. With his comrades in the Black Consciousness Movement, they left us a legacy that teaches us that what we think about ourselves, how we feel, how we function in the world can be unlearned. Psychological liberation matters.

We need psychological liberation from violent masculinities and the cult of femininity – to learn to engage as partners across genders, to respect women's bodily autonomy and entitlement to

69

sexual and other pleasures. We need to disown violence everywhere except in self-defence.

I started out by linking silence in our gender-talk to violent masculinities and the cult of femininity. We cannot re-shape patriarchy without an honest look at our society, our language and our everyday practice. As Black people, we have relearned how to love our hair textures, our varied tones, our hips, our sounds, our creative legacies, and, in the main, how to take other Black people seriously. We can learn how to value freedom even when we are not under attack. We are not going to get very far, however, if we ignore history, since how we deal with our history has everything to do with who we are and can be. That is part of the powerful legacy that the Black Consciousness Movement bestowed on us.

But history is very untidy, so working through it is even more hard work. Those in the Lesbian, Gay, Bisexual, Transgender, intersex, Queer (LGBTiQ) movement know that this is true too, because the experience of living in a homophobic society makes it hard work to love your gender non-conforming, same-sex, same-gender-loving self.

However, if we choose not to embark on this road, we may as well give up on our Constitution and that beautiful self-loving and self-valuing vision that it offers us.

When we talk about how gloriously revolutionary the 1980s were, we are right. But what are the connections between the down-playing of women's roles in the struggle and what the experience of that role was? To revisit the history of activism means taking seriously the fact that women had experiences that sometimes complicated narrow retellings of the struggle. This is not just true of the 1980s. However, I start with the 1980s because of what else young Black women – lesbian, straight, bisexual – were experiencing in addition to sexist and racist state brutality. Whatever we may want to use as a lens to explain jackrolling in Transvaal townships, which was pervasive, or the rise of iintsara as part of the gendered gang violence of the Cape Flats, these cannot continue to be moments we gloss over.

Ingrid Masondo pointed out in an interview recently that ignoring this phase of our collective history throws away those many, many Black women who were kidnapped and gang-raped over a period of a decade in urban areas, and a longer period in rural areas. This complicates commonplace feminist arguments that hold that most women are sexually violated by men they know, and that consequently, stranger-danger presents a small part of the problem. In South Africa, for successive generations of Black women, the fear of public abduction by strange men was not just real but also very likely. We make these women disposable citizens when we pretend this era away.

"What happens to that collective trauma?" Masondo asks. It is a chilling question.

What happens to the collective trauma of ukuthwalwa, being jackrolled or falling prey to iintsara? Most of those women are alive today. Explanations of this as state-sponsored, Black-on-Black violence are unhelpful because they do not tell us how to deal with that collective traumatisation, that incessant communication to us in our formative years that as Black women we do not have freedom of movement. That communication is reinforced by the statistics today, and recently by drama such as the incredibly damaging masculinist posturing around the Jacob Zuma rape trial.

As a teenager, although I had never been to Cape Town and had only briefly been to one township in what was then the Transvaal, news and details of the exploits of jackrolling in the Transvaal gangs and iintsara that terrorised Cape Town townships from their base in Nyanga East reached far and wide. The women I went to school with in both Inanda Seminary on the outskirts of Durban, and All Saints Senior College near Bhisho spoke with terror of jackrollers and iintsara. Writing about how iintsara captured the public imagination even in the fraught 1980s township life in Cape Town, Sandile Dikeni calls iintsara gangsters a "strangely organised" criminal phenomenon and "one of their most testing experiences" of 1980s Cape Town, and how iintsara and similar gangs retained a firmer grip on the memory of the time than even the brutal "witdoeke, a notorious cop called Barnard, or

71

some of the vigilante forces in what is called, for want of a better description, the taxi industry."

For Dikeni, it was the combination of political apathy and the rise of crime that enabled iintsara to rise as they did. He relates an encounter with them thus:

> it was a common sight to watch iiNtsara marching in some disorganised way down some main road in Nyanga East brandishing every kind of weapon imaginable. In one of these exhibitions of gang power, I had the unpleasant opportunity to witness the false sense of authority that gangsterism and mob psychology grants young people. This particular march was led by a thug called uTyhopho. Tyhopho was a young boy, who earned his flamboyancy by undressing himself to the waist and making extremely strange noises and blood curdling ululations while he led his troop of nearly a hundred or so 'skepsels' who felt absolutely untouchable. In this crazy spell, Tyhopho, brandishing some quite dangerous looking dagger, would momentarily stop, throw himself to the ground mutter some more of his strange words, and then roll to the pavement and start sharpening his assegai to the absolute glee of his followers.

Iintsara obviously understood the power of public performance of power and terror. How could they not, growing up as Black people in townships where the state performed terror publicly through presence, public patrolling, shootings, beatings, abductions, tear-gas and other forms of terrorising communities? And of course, like other gangsters, rape was simply one of a range of criminal and violent ways in which iinstara operated. As Dikeni shows, the rise of iintsara was also decidedly opposed to organised activism in such townships, and interestingly, it was activists who ultimately rid Nyanga East of the gangsters through violent means that were nonetheless self-defence.

How horribly ironic for women whose foremothers marched on the Union Buildings decades before.

An accompanying question needs to be asked, what happened

to all those young men who were jackrollers or iintsara? In what ways did being able to get away with mass rape solidify violent masculine patterns, and what kind of socialisation did it have on other Black men and boys watching? What (unintended) consequences for masculinities and femininities followed from this?

How much of what has become normal has some roots here? How does another history of sanctioned women's kidnapping – ukuthwala – contribute to the possibility of jackrolling being normal? At which point do we take responsibility for unlearning harmful behaviour regardless of which part of our complicated history it comes from? At which point do violent men in this country, and the women who are their cronies, women Desiree Lewis has called 'phallic women', stop using 'culture' as a way to justify violating us?

We know that today women do not feel safe in the streets and homes of South Africa, that women's bodies are seen as accessible for consumption – touching, raping, kidnapping, commenting on, grabbing, twisting, beating, burning, maiming – and control, that women are denied the very freedom that 'empowerment' suggests, the very freedom the Constitution protects. And the problem is often made women's responsibility. The police warn women drivers to yield at a red robot and drive on when we feel unsafe at night, to be extra vigilant when we approach a robot and see young Black men approaching, or to avoid travelling alone. In other words, privileged women should take responsibility for the fact that we/they may be attacked at any time and modify our behaviour accordingly. Less-privileged women who rely on public transport are warned not to be out in deserted areas, encouraged to dress conservatively, and to avoid the front seat of a taxi. Again, the message is clear: women, modify your behaviour, and adjust all aspects of your life in the unlikely chance that you might avoid falling prey to serial killers or other gender-based violence.

These warnings do not work, and they are dangerous warnings at that, because they communicate quite unequivocally that South

African public spaces do not belong to the women who live in this country. They are the same messages that iintsara and jackrollers and those who engaged in ukuthwala communicated to the 45 per cent majority that is Black women in this country and, in this regard, they were in line with apartheid state-sponsored terror. They communicate this quite clearly: you had better make yourself seem safe in order to be safe – stay at home, participate in the cult of femininity, give in to unwanted sexual advances, surrender many choices, make yourselves as small, quiet and invisible as possible.

But in the true style of all patriarchy's promises, they lie, because South African women are saying we cannot escape gender-based violence even when we play by the rules of the cult of femininity. South African women and girls are saying that across sexual orientation, in the classrooms of urban and rural South Africa, on the streets of our cities and towns, as well as in the fields and homes of our rural areas, in buses, taxis, trains and private cars, in shopping malls, cafés, factories and hospitals. The statistics support us, and the criminal justice system either re-violates or ignores us.

And all the while gender-conservative men threaten and violently silence women who speak out in self-defence against a former vice-president in 2006 – now state president in 2015 – and women's votes helped elect him, despite his misogyny about what women want when we dress a certain way, act a certain way.

There is clear and urgent need to change South Africa's public and private gender-talk. We need to tackle violent masculinities head on, exposing the disdain with which violent men hold all women. As part of this we need to rid ourselves of the 'passwords' that Sibongile Ndashe speaks about in "Can I speak, please!", which refer to the disclaimers and qualifiers that silence real debate on gender-based violence.

Ndashe says these passwords are a pre-requisite that goes something akin to "not all men are rapists, and that in the past some people have been falsely accused."

Continuing to mouth these passwords, and demanding them

before you listen to what women have to say, is part of the problem. A significant part of the discourse on gender-based violence requires such passwords, which, by their very existence, prevent us from finding a way out of the siege. So, those Black and white feminists who defied the passwords by contesting the gender-talk around the Jacob Zuma trial were dismissed as 'elites', 'irresponsible', 'disingenuous', and out of touch with most poor women, who are coyly called 'real women on the ground'.

It is an incredible statement coming from elite men, and amazingly condescending, since these men, we are to assume, know better what women want. These passwords bar access to a hearing by a 'general' audience. But who is it that makes up this 'general' audience? Patriarchal women and opportunistic men, conservative men and women who think that claiming that there is a conspiracy justifies making Black women's bodies expendable battlegrounds. Gender-conservative South African men would do well to choose another battleground because claiming that women who call them on their misogyny do not speak as 'real' South African women is direct complicity with the scourge of gender-based violence that is upon us. These 'general' audience members sit proudly among those who are determined to make women's entitlement to bodily integrity and autonomy impossible. They hold us hostage. It is on their feet especially that I lay the gauntlet of rethinking and unlearning their own violent masculinities. It is they, too, and sometimes, they *especially*, who must be vigilant in the face of how the gendering of their identities is part of what makes violence normal.

They must contribute to gender-progressive efforts to ensure that women are economically empowered in ways that alter the South African landscape and "eradicate patriarchal myths that nurture the delusions of grandeur and power that so many men suffer from and that encourage this grotesque sense of entitlement", in the words of Elaine Salo, in her presentation at the Harold Wolpe Memorial Trust Open Dialogue Event. It is not enough for leaders of political formations of various sorts to mouth commitment to gender equity when they excuse misogyny spoken in their midst.

It is irresponsible and violent for them to defend violence against women.

We need gender-transformative education that is not left only in the classroom, but also alters how we parent, ensuring that it is the responsibility of everyone – not just women – to expose, disown and hold accountable those men who act violently towards women and children.

After our collective witnessing of the unfolding of events around the Zuma rape trial, I hope we reflect more critically on how to do the work of resisting and unlearning violent masculinities and dissociating ourselves from the cult of femininity. As I have said before, and will say again, the Jacob Zuma rape trial, and the incredible brutality it invited in his male and female supporters, held a mirror to our faces. As those who work towards the end of gender-based violence know, the case was typical of rape cases in most ways. It and its defendant were not exceptional except in that the case magnified how society and the legal justice system act in such cases.

Perhaps it brought us to a crisis point, and we can choose to learn from it, and do the hard work we all need to do. I hope we come closer to working towards the kind of society our Constitution says we can be, by doing the hard work that will bring us psychological liberation and ultimately gender equity. The current situation makes a mockery of the values of the Constitution. But choosing different behaviour can bring us closer to a society in which the gender values of the Constitution are entrenched.

Would it not be a wonderful thing, if this was the legacy we left our younger siblings, and our actual or symbolic children and grandchildren? To leave behind a society that makes sense when read against the Constitution and the Women's March? A society that really takes everyone's humanity seriously, that does not restrict freedom of movement for its women and girls, a country that protects each woman's, man's or transgender person's right to choice and association, a country in which a trial such as the Jacob Zuma rape trial is impossible?

It would be an amazing thing if, waking up in 2056, South African girls and women really had freedom of movement, as passes – actual and more slippery passwords – were a fact relegated to history books.

This is not an impossible legacy, and indeed, it is an urgent future to build.

CHAPTER 4

The female fear factory

The female fear factory is as theatrical as it is spectacular. By theatrical, I allude to its exaggerated performance in front of an audience in terms that are immediately understood. It is spectacular in its reliance on visible, audible and other recognisable cues to transmit fear and to control. Performed regularly in public spaces and mediated forms, it is both mythologised, sometimes though a language of respectability and at other times through shame.

In his essay "Rediscovery of the Ordinary", Njabulo Ndebele describes the spectacular as that which prioritises the obvious, and retains its grip on the imagination long after the encounter has passed. The spectacular is also about communicating power and legitimacy. He writes that "[w]hat matters is what is seen. Thinking is secondary to seeing. Subtlety is secondary to obviousness. What is finally left and what is deeply etched in our minds is the spectacular contest between the powerless and the powerful."

The female fear factory, which I also call the manufacture of female fear, relies on quick, effective transfer of meaning.

To normalise depends on a combination of seemingly contradictory processes: frequent repetition of performance until the performance becomes invisible. In other words, when we see and hear something over and over again, we stop seeing and hearing it. It retreats to the background where, like static becoming white noise, we come to expect it. We come to expect it in a process of partial desensitisation. Once this happens its interruption becomes strange, dangerous and often unthinkable.

The manufacture of female fear uses the threat of rape and other bodily wounding but sometimes mythologises this violence as benefit. Under capitalism work is codified as respectability. Those who are without work are shamed while those who work are said to have dignity. To want to work redeems the worker from a fate of uselessness, dependency and laziness. Those who seek to take the factory apart, want to determine compensation or want to own their labour are demonised.

Like a real factory, it takes up public physical space, requires many bodies and different components. Like an assembly line, it involves movement with the addition of components as the belt moves seamlessly from post to post. It is a machine set to work in one direction and one that could injure those who get in the way. Interfering promises injury to any body parts that attempt to interfere with the process. It needs a power source and is a very effective process of production. Its products are for ready consumption and although harmful it finds such high circulation that it seems normal. Although the product is female fear, its products are generalised fear in all audiences.

The threat of rape is an effective way to remind women that they are not safe and that their bodies are not entirely theirs. It is an exercise in power that communicates that the man creating fear has power over the woman who is the target of his attention; it also teaches women who witness it about their vulnerability either through reminding them of their own previous fear or showing them that it could happen to them next. It is an effective way to keep women in check and often results in women curtailing their movement in a physical and psychological manner.

The manufacture of female fear works to silence women by reminding us of our rapability, and therefore blackmails us to keep ourselves in check. It also sometimes works to remind some men and trans-people that they are like women, and therefore also rapable. It is a public fear that is repeatedly manufactured through various means in many private and public settings. This chapter, on the female fear factory explores the many sites wherein female fear is manufactured. South Africa's public culture is infused with this phenomenon.

The manufacture of female fear requires several aspects to work: the safety of the aggressor, the vulnerability of the target, the successful communication by the aggressor that he has power to wound, rape and/or kill the target with no consequences to himself. Women are socialised to look away from the female fear factory – to pretend it is not happening and to flee when ignoring it becomes impossible. Patriarchy trains us all to be receptive to the conditions that produce – and reproduce – female fear, especially when it is not our own bodies on the assembly line.

Examples illustrate best, they can work as evidence, and it is to four examples that I now turn for recognition and illumination.

In the winter of 2013, feminist Lebo Pule shared a story about being in a shop in the Johannesburg CBD where a young man harassed a young woman. It is a familiar site where violence, gender and sexuality rub up against one another. As Pule looks on, the young man tries to get the young woman's attention by calling out to her, addressing her in increasingly direct ways. When she continues to ignore him, his aggression grows, he starts to goad her.

Although she does not utter any words, she communicates her disinterest in his attention through her body language, a language that is recognisable to Pule and the other spectators in the shop, and also one clearly understood by the young man in pursuit. She does not speak back. When he persists, she walks away, all the while refusing to return his gaze.

In various ways hers is an attempt to pretend he is not there, to wish him away and to create distance between them. This clearly communicates that his attention is unwelcome. When she realises that none of this will have the intended effect, the young woman turns around and pointedly informs him that she is not interested in talking to him and that he should leave her alone. She tells him to go away.

He says, "That is why we rape you."

An enraged Pule intervenes, interrogates the man asking him first, "How is that why you rape women?", and then "How many women have you raped?"

Increasingly the rest of the shop watches in slight shock at Pule's confrontation of the young man. They find her behaviour strange, are surprised that she intervened and will not let it go, making the young man uncomfortable.

They are so accustomed to this kind of behaviour that it is not the young man's threats that are strange, but Pule's refusal to let him continue.

The shopkeepers keep quiet.

The harassed young woman turns around and tries to console and reassure Pule, telling her "Don't get yourself so worked up, my sister, we're used to these dogs speaking like this to us. They are rubbish."

Various versions of this story play themselves out in public spaces several times a day. At the same time, there are specific special aspects to this particular incident. The first is the refusal of the young man to take 'no' for an answer. While the woman knows his is a refusal rather than a misunderstanding, she is determined to communicate her 'no' in various ways, with increasing levels of assertiveness. She is unequivocal. He cannot claim to have misunderstood. At the same time, the young woman knows that she is not safe even in this public place with several other people present. Consequently, she tries to escape first his gaze by looking away and pretending not to hear him. When this attempted symbolic escape fails, she tries to escape again by walking away, moving away from the unwanted attention.

If she is determined to reassert her refusal, he is determined to remind her of its insignificance. She cannot escape and he knows this. In case she does not know it, he will remind her. With increasing aggression, he reminds her that she cannot get away from unwanted attention, that he feels entitled to her time, her mind and her body. When she tells him to go away, he reminds her that he does not care about what she wants. She does not matter. She is not entitled to her body. He is entitled to everything: her attention, her body, and everyone's eyes and ears in the shop.

The directness of his allusion to rape is the finishing touch. He will have her regardless of what she wants. He reminds her of his complete power and her powerlessness. The use of the plural is particularly striking here because it renders in explicit, crude language publicly what often appears only by implication: both he and she belong to types, are representative. It is the ultimate expression of men's entitlement to women's bodies: she can surrender to his advances or she can be made to submit. Either way, he has power over her.

Equally instructive is the freedom and safety this man feels to be the aggressor and to express his threat of violence in full view of various other people. His safety relies on her vulnerability. No challenge to his power will be effective, he seems to be saying. He is secure in his power over her, and others like her, because he has the conviction of repetition: nothing will happen to him, even in a shop full of people.

Pule's response is startling because it interrupts this manufacture of female fear. Unlike the other shoppers, she will not remain silent. Unlike the shopkeepers, she is not cowered. The interruption of the female fear factory assembly line is strange because it deviates from what has become normal.

The young man is stunned into silence for the first time since the encounter started. The element of surprise disarms him so effectively that he not only remains silent, but he ultimately leaves. He is surprised by the interrupted conveyer belt, by Pule's spanner in the works. Pule's outburst is revealingly rendered as a string of questions. She quite literally questions his behaviour; to question is to render strange, abnormal.

The behaviour of the other people in the shop is also revealing of what enables the repeated performance of the threats of violence against women in public. They act predictably by not coming to the woman's defence but by pretending not to see. It is this averted gaze that normalises public performances of violence and threats of rape specifically. If people will pretend not to see, he has freedom to violate, and he says as much in his parting shot.

He cannot foresee Pule's actions to render him unsafe, to curtail his freedom to violate. This is why the spectators are also stunned by Pule: she seems unafraid. The conveyer belt has been interrupted.

This is what the young woman also confirms when she comforts Pule, referring to how pervasive this threatening behaviour is as well as in trying to convince Pule not to be too upset. The young woman refuses the normal, but she recognises that Pule rejects the aggression as normal. In other words, she exhibits an ambivalence that is striking: although not compliant herself, she is not quite as outraged as Pule is. What the exchange between the two women also illustrates is reciprocity. Pule's actions are in defence of the young woman, rendering the aggressor unsafe and fortifying the young woman's resistance. She responds aggressively towards the aggressor and helpfully towards the target. The young woman, in turn, recognises this and attempts to make Pule feel better. If Pule's gesture communicates to the young woman that she is not alone, the young woman's response to Pule is recognition of this solidarity and a return of the demonstrated care.

It is a strangeness that stuns the aggressor, rendering him unsafe as Pule will not be complicit. The safety of the aggressor lies in the absence of consequence, in a complicit and cowered audience, and a target that behaves appropriately: ignoring, shrinking, cowering.

A story such as this one highlights various things about the working of the female fear factory. When the man targets the young woman with increasing levels of aggression, he knows that although others feel uncomfortable and possibly disapprove of his actions, they will do nothing. She knows this too, and this is why she initially attempts to make herself invisible, to shrink. However, even when she decides to defend herself and responds by telling him to leave her alone, nobody comes to her aid. Helen Moffett has demonstrated a similar process in her essay "These women, they force us to rape them", where she shows how rape functions as a very clearly understood tool of gendered social control of a gendered and raced Other. Although Moffett's essay has even more relevance for an earlier chapter in this book, I find her formulation of this social control as "an unacknowledged gender civil war" quite apt here. The young woman in Pule's story knows she is under attack from this young man and others like him. Yet, the averted gaze means there is no one on her side as the other shoppers behave predictably. In Pule's absence, nothing would mediate these acts of gender warfare against her. Moffett's essay title also has obvious connections to Pule's story; her quotation of a rape "justificatory narrative" rhymes with the words of the man in Pule's story. In that moment, she knows that she is in real danger of attack, and that nobody will likely come to her aid. He knows this too.

The other women in the shop know this too. Although they would undoubtedly appreciate someone coming to their aid when they are harassed in public, they do not act as they would have someone act in their defence. Consequently, a single man is able to hold several people hostage, all of them afraid of what he might do if they confront him.

When he threatens her with rape, it is the worst form of lashing out he can imagine. He knows that rape is something women will do anything to avoid, even as they know they cannot. He is also demonstrating his absolute power over her, the fact that she belongs nowhere and he everywhere. When he says "This is why we rape you," he communicates his total power over her. Unlike him, she has no choices, he communicates. She can surrender to one form of harassment or be subjected to another. Either way, she will be violated.

Pule's reaction ruptures this veneer of absolute power and shames the young man as violator who threatens even more violence. And, unlike what the others suspect, he retreats. He does not know how to deal with such unpredictable behaviour. He does not attempt to control Pule too. He leaves the shop. Pule's example suggests that one of the ways to change his attitude, and those of others in the shop, is to interrupt the manufacture of female fear, rather than to cower to it. She refuses to 'mind her own business' and decides to contest his power by coming to the aid of the young woman who resists. She defeats the young man because she is uncovered.

The second story is that of Anene Booysen, the story of a young woman's betrayal, rape and murder. On 2 February 2013, Anene Booysen, a 17-year-old woman from Bredasdorp in the Western Cape was raped and disembowelled after leaving a tavern close to her home with the young man who would later be convicted of her rape and murder, whom she had known as her brother's peer. Discovered in a pool of her own blood with her intestines hanging outside her body, she was left for dead at a construction site not too far from her home. Her friend, Monisha Ruiters was quoted in Kate Stegeman's "Remembering Anene Booysen: The sound, the fury and the politicking", published in the *Mail and Guardian*, 11 February 2013, as having said *"Dit kan met enige een van ons nou gebeur. Dit was vir ons kinders 'n voorbeeld vir ons dat ons nie so laat loop nie.* [This could happen to any one of us. This was an example for us children that we mustn't walk around so late at night."]

Booysen's story is devastating in many ways because it is a story that highlights how elusive safety is for women. Booysen went to drink at a tavern that is in the same area she has lived for most of her life. It is located in her community, among people she has lived with, whose names she knows. She drank with people she knows, not the strangers that girls are often told to avoid in an effort to remain safe from harm. She followed the script given to girls and young women about safety – she did not go too far away, and when she chose to drink, she did so with people she knows by name. When she eventually left the tavern, she did so with someone who is her brother's peer, someone who was to act as proxy for her brother.

Booysen made sure not to leave alone, a decision she knew would put her at risk. She did what girls are told to do: she left with a familiar man with whom she had a relationship, a man who would signal her protection to other men in public at night. She tried to protect herself by not making herself vulnerable. She knows women are supposed to be afraid to walk home alone at night – she had learnt this lesson of fearing freedom.

She had done all the right things for women who are out at night: left with a known man as possible protection. Women are routinely told that to be out without the possibility of male protection at night renders them vulnerable to rape, attack and murder.

In Anene Booysen's story, the terrorisation, breaking of her body and ending of her life seemed almost unbelievable in the sheer repetition of its violence. Throughout the country, people gathered together to commemorate her life, mourn her and reflect on what her rape and murder meant. There were candlelight memorials, marches, Fridays in which calls went out that we dress in white and others in black, and many other initiatives to mark this moment in the young woman's life, her death and what it sometimes means to be a young woman in South Africa.

Her death was terrifying and heartbreaking, and in many places people came together to testify to this. Some of the questions raised by her rape and murder remain. But there was also something else that reveals much about the psyche of South Africa and the female fear factory.

There was a frenzy to apportion blame on a range of people close to her. She was blamed for being in the wrong place at the wrong time, drinking out at night, walking the streets at night, all behaviour that patriarchy says is inappropriate for good girls. Sometimes callers to radio stations expressed a combination of shock and attempts to explain how such a thing could happen by slut-shaming and victim-blaming her. Her judgment was questioned by some who then quickly and condescendingly decided that her class standing meant she did not know better. Several others argued that this kind of brutality is what poverty reduces people to, thereby explaining away the responsibility that her attackers, rapists and murderers had. As days passed, the bizarre focus on the layers of supposed responsibility that everybody should have taken intensified: her parents, her foster parents who let her go out at night and loved her so imperfectly that the only picture of her that was circulated initially was her ID photo, Anene who should not have gone out at night, the community that allowed this to happen, the business owners of the premises from which she was taken, the father who did not protect her adequately. Everybody but the men who tormented, raped, slaughtered and killed her were blamed.

On 11 February, Ferial Haffajee wrote a column "#WTF was she thinking?" in which she spoke of the fear she imagined Anene must have felt, a fear she could identify with as a young woman, the constant awareness of being at risk and the factors that ensured her safety. She wrote:

> When I read Anene Booysen's story, I was stunned by my journalistic retardation and my instinctive identification with her passport sized photograph. [...] The fear of attack was like my shadow growing up. Walks home from school were always made with eyes sharply strained, backwards, forward, backward.

Haffajee points to the pervasiveness of female fear, that she recognises what happened to Anene Booysen as the horror that all girls are reared to fear. This excerpt also shows that girls are taught to fear being in public places no matter what time it is: Haffajee would be in uniform, straight from school and still afraid of attack and rape. Later, in the same piece, Haffajee asks "Tell me Anene Booysen's life might not have turned out differently with better safeguards?"

But even as she asks this question, Haffajee knows that women cannot guarantee their safety, that no safeguards by parents or teachers or ourselves promise escape from the fear and the very real possibility of being attacked in public.

This is a follow up on her editorial published a day earlier as "Editor's note: Words fail us" in which she mentions the fact that Anene Booysen's foster mother had provided her ID picture, about which she now writes:

[t]he photograph looks like Anene was not a kid whose every life step was photographed. It looks like the only photograph ever taken of her – unlike loved children who are constantly captured on camera for posterity by adoring parents. [...] That's clue one.

Haffejee has many questions:

Would Anene's destiny have been different with firm guiding hands of loving, doting, focused parents? Or would she only have been safe in a country where rape is not sport?

Haffajee credits various things that kept her, unlike Anene Booysen, safe: her protective, loving parents who watched her and brought her up properly and ensured that she did not 'go wild' with curfews, and her ADT security service and high walls as an adult. All of these mark her as very differently protected from Anene who "did not have parents of her own" as well as that "the young men who violated and killed her were also not cosseted and loved, to bring them to human wholeness and into a decent adulthood."

Haffajee's stance here is quite astounding, not least because of who she is, and her consistent writing against gendered violence in the past. She knows that loving your children does not protect them from harm. Cossetted children are molested all over the world, sometimes by people who should protect them. Anene Booysen's foster parents chose her and took care of her as best they could. They had to deal with the guilt of inadequacy that plagues even those parents who photograph their children obsessively.

To be sure, Haffajee is no rape apologist, as her record of anti-rape writing clearly shows. Yet, her stance on Booysen as evinced in these two columns is an interesting commentary on the workings of the female fear factory. On the one hand, Haffajee recognises that fear is a huge part of being in public spaces as a woman. She names it the shadow that followed her and her friends everywhere as a child, ever aware of the possibility of attack, watchful. She recognises that this continues to be a fear for many women in public today, a fear that is constantly reinforced by various predatory men known and unknown – like the taxi driver that frightens the young woman she starts her second column in conversation with, and the young mandrax-smoking men in her building as a child. On the other hand, she argues that safety is a possibility for children with adequately structured and loving parenting.

Here was a scripting of rape blame as belonging to a whole range of people already traumatised by Anene Booysen's fate in a classic case of misplaced anger. Anene Booysen was both victim and shamed. But her foster mother did not rape and slaughter her. Furthermore, in a country where violence against women is indeed a 'sport' in which men from all backgrounds participate in alarming numbers, the class background of Booysen's murderers is not a convincing mitigating factor.

There are several named instances of the female fear factor in this story. First is the fear Anene Booysen felt herself, the fear she sought to mitigate by choosing a companion to walk home with. Second is the fear she must have felt when she realised that she was about to be raped and killed. Third is the fear she must have felt abandoned on that construction site, alone, when the worst had happened. Fourth is the fear her foster mother must have felt not knowing where her child was. Fear for the safety of your children is such a constitutive part of mothering in patriarchal society, and especially one as violent as our country. Fifth is the fear Haffajee speaks of – both the fear she felt as a young woman feeling vulnerable to attack by known and unknown men in public, and the fear she manages as an adult middle-class woman with various safety features in her home and car.

Finally, Monisha Ruiters understands the language of the female fear factory. Not only has she lost her friend, raped and killed by men they both know, but she has to face her own trauma and grief without reprieve from the manufacture of female fear. She notes that she too is unsafe, that all of them are unsafe. This could happen to one of them. It already has – Anene is one of them. But even this must be a lesson in the spectacular communication of the manufacture of female fear. It is a warning about what could happen if they continue to walk around late at night, even in their own community. The lesson on adjusting women's behaviour and giving up access to public spaces is well communicated.

The third story is the story of a very special thirty-one-year-old woman who should have been the pride and joy of our country and her community. Eudy Simelane was a gifted midfielder who played for Banyana Banyana, the national women's soccer team, and an LGBTi activist.

Simelane was robbed, stripped, gang-raped, stabbed twelve times and killed the day after Freedom Day in 2008 in her home township of KwaThema, Gauteng, in what was recognised as a hate crime, and the targeting of Simelane because she was an out lesbian. She was not safe in her own township, her community as a woman, and was open to attack because even sports stars are unsafe when they are women. No amount of glory protects a woman from attack and rape and brutal murder.

There are many similarities between Simelane and Booysen even if they lived in different parts of the country. They were raped and killed by members of their own community, and their bodies mutilated in particularly horrific ways afterwards. They were treated in this manner in the very places they called home, by men they knew.

For an out lesbian, KwaThema is a particularly disturbing place for a hate crime. This is because KwaThema had an established, known and celebrated gay-subculture, where in the 1980s there were various expressions of out LGBTiQ expression in public as well as an established out community.

Such attacks on women, and on women who are out lesbians – even in spaces where they should feel safe – communicates the perpetual danger women face in public spaces. It is a reminder that they should be afraid, no matter where they are, afraid because they are women and afraid because they are women who love women.

The female fear factory also appeared as Themba Mvubu was seen muttering "I'm not sorry" as he left court after being convicted of Simelane's murder and as accomplice to her rape. In court, it had earlier been revealed that Mvubu had instructed his co-accused Thato Mphiti to kill Simelane since she knew him and would therefore be able to identify him. This absence of remorse was notable since Mvubu's role in the abduction had been established, as had the fact that he knew Simelane.

At an earlier point in the criminal case, charges had been dropped against Tsepo Pitja, accused number four, the man who had fetched Simelane from her home prior to her gang rape, robbery and murder, much to the frustration of activists who applied pressure on the state to see the trial through. Such pressure had been necessary after several delays from various arms of the State including the Director of Public Prosecutions, the South African Police Services and the Prosecutor. In a public march organised by the Lesbian and Gay Equality Project and KwaThema community organisations and residents on 10 September 2008, the activists demanded "a thorough investigation" while raising "concerns over the DPP in referring the matter to the High Court" and insisting "that the Prosecutor make efficient consultations with the other two agents." One of these activists is quoted in the 7 October 2008 statement issued by this group as saying "He knows most of us. He is a known rapist and now we are scared that he will be outside and target us like they did to Eudy."

The lack of remorse by Mvubu and charges being dropped against Pitja contribute to a context where women's lives are unsafe and undervalued. Both knew Simelane, and she trusted one of them enough to leave home with him. Furthermore, that the criminal case of such a prominent woman had to be so closely guarded and activists had to apply constant pressure reinforces the disregard for women's lives within the criminal justice system as much as in broader society. While women are rendered unsafe in their communities, and are constantly reminded of this, including by seeing a man who is 'a known rapist', justice remains elusive for many. Under such conditions, fear becomes the shadow that accompanies women in public spaces in precisely the ways Haffajee outlined above.

Eudy Simelane's case was not an isolated case. Wendy Isaack, writing in the Lesbian and Gay Equality Project pamphlet, "A state of emergency: hate crimes against Black lesbians" in 2002, noted that:

> [h]ate crimes against Black lesbians must not be seen as a separate and distinct phenomenon from the high incidence of gender-based violence in this country. There are differences in so far as sexual orientation is concerned, yet before one is a lesbian, one is a woman. Her sexual orientation may nevertheless pose added difficulties and challenges in respect of her ability to access resources and services. On a daily basis lesbians are subjected to violence including rape in the belief that it will cure them of their sexual orientation. It is important to stress that patriarchal societies have always aimed to define and dominate female sexuality and self-determination. Women who live a self-determined sexuality challenge this man-centred system. In this respect, violence against lesbians is clearly linked to violence against women and to a world-wide patriarchal attitude.

The manufacture of female fear is concerned with regulating women's movement, sexuality and behaviour. What has been dubbed 'curative' or 'corrective' rape is a manifestation of this desire to control, monitor and police all aspects of women's lives. Lesbian women are marked as inappropriately sexual and the motivation or justification for raping and/or killing them often surfaces the desire to render them heterosexual. However, women assumed to be heterosexual are raped and/or killed at alarming rates. While lesbians are targeted in specific and regular instances, they are also to be rendered fearful of living their lives on their terms, in a collision of patriarchal and homophobic power that lies behind rapist men's senses of entitlement to women's bodies.

The fourth story is drawn from the work of Diana Russell. It is the story of a woman who chose the pseudonym Lulu Diba, who keeps news of her rape more than a decade earlier from her boyfriends out of fear. Here, the manufacture of female fear is effected in ways that make Diba regulate information in order to self-protect. It is also evident in other ways in her story as the narrative reveals.

Asked why she conceals news of her rape from partners, she responds:

> Our men want us to be pure, so I never tell any of my boyfriends that I was raped. The problem is not about my losing my virginity. It is that being raped leaves a stigma. People do not sympathise with you. Instead they say you wanted it. Any black man who knows that I have been raped would lose interest in me.

This trauma from her past is suppressed as a way of managing the fear of being undesirable to partners. Rape, in this case, is seen as stigma that contaminates rather than inviting empathy. If she desires companionship, then, she has to disown this part of herself, fearful of the further damage it will cause in her present life.

Lulu Diba was raped by an acquaintance at university, at a party, during which his friends slapped and then tried to catch her as she ran away, half naked. A woman friend came upon the scene and disrupted the chain of events. It is one of those rare rapes where there were witnesses and such evidence was available. At the same time, speaking about her rape led to secondary victimisation by various people who were supposed to assist her in her recovery.

The first secondary victimiser was the Afrikaner District Surgeon about whom Diba reveals, "He said he was sick and tired of students being so careless. He said we asked to be raped and that we are not supposed to walk alone at night."

Her second was a police sergeant to whom she reported the case. Diba continues:

> The police sergeant was even worse. He told me that he would also like to have 'a taste.' '*I will come to your room*', he said. '*I will be gentle with you*'. I cried because I was so surprised and upset by his saying these things. He was a black man of about my age, so I expected sympathy from him.

93

At a student meeting the following week, two of the rapist's friends in the same course as Diba admitted that they had witnessed him rape her but denied that slapping and chasing her was an attempt to rape her too. She chose to have the Disciplinary Committee of the University handle matters and dropped the police case:

> because I wanted to avoid the questioning in court as well as publicity about being raped. I feared that news of the rape would reach my father's ears. My father is very strict and he would have been very hurt to know I had been raped.

She had to endure constant stigma and actual taunting by the rapist and his friends, ongoing interviews by lecturers in the Social Work department even though they were not part of the investigation, with professionals who are supposed to assist, choosing to add yet another layer of secondary victimisation.

Although the perpetrator admitted to raping her, he also claimed she enjoyed it and since her friend had only seen the aftermath and his friends would not act as witnesses, he was not disciplined. This meant that as Diba continued with her degree for two more years, she frequently encountered her rapist and his friends on the small university campus.

This compounded trauma has meant that eleven years later, when she narrates the story to Diana Russell, Diba still battles to speak about it to people she might lose. She informs Russell:

> [t]o this day, the rape is still my secret. Because I was blamed for it at the time, I always think people will be judgmental if I tell them. Sometimes I say to my girl friend, *'I've got something I want to share with you'*. She says, *'What is it?'* Then I tell her something else. I haven't even told my sisters. [...] I am very protective of myself because I don't want to be hurt again, so I don't become very involved in my relationships. I have good relationships with women and men who aren't my boyfriends.

Lulu Diba speaks of other rapes that were managed differently at her university, such as that of a woman raped by her boyfriend who did not report it as rape. She speaks as well of 'test matches', the name given to gang rapes at the university:

> Test matches involved a girl's boyfriend inviting her to visit him. When she accepted, he would put brake fluid in her drink which would knock her out. Then he and his friends would rape her. They did this to girls for very petty reasons; for example, if a woman's boyfriend thought she was too stubborn or that she felt she was too high for him. This was a way of punishing her, of bringing her down.

Commenting on Lulu Diba's experience at a South African university, Diana Russell notes that rape culture is widespread at university campuses in the US where the equivalent of 'test matches' is common. She also reminds us that "[d]enigrating survivors also discourages others from reporting." It also creates and reinforces a culture of fear for women who have access to this information, as well as to other rape survivors.

Lulu Diba's story has layers of fear. Because of her experience when she told the story to a range of people who should have come to her aid, as well as the fact that she was repeatedly blamed, slut-shamed and taunted, she fears further, similar repercussions. She also knows that her experience is not isolated, and names other women at her campus who did not report their rapes for fear that they would also be shamed, blamed and taunted.

Rape culture trivialises the experience of rape, reducing it to sex and denying harm. It also uses various techniques to trivialise specific rapes as well as all rape. Writing of her experience at the Mitchells Plain Crisis Line, Dawn Adams notes the similarities between the shame felt by clients around battery, incest and rape. She continues:

[t]he rape survivor invariably feels that what happened to her is at least partly her fault. She is then scared to speak out, due to feelings of guilt, and sometimes might fear retribution. Another problem we face here is dealing with the stigma attached to this crime, which causes so many perpetrators of this violent crime to go free.

If women fear that they will be punished for being raped and for speaking about it, and they see evidence of this repeatedly in how other women who survive are treated, it makes sense that although many go for counselling, they may choose not to report it to the police.

I could narrate many more stories. But we all know stories of rape and fear. Many of us live them directly and indirectly. Rape is the threat that the manufacture of female fear promises if we do not keep each other, and ourselves in check. At the same time, the enactment of rape reinforces this fear. When we see other women experience it, and when they are further victimised for having survived it, fear is reinforced.

The female fear factory is a lesson in subjugation. Yet, it does not fully succeed because it is sometimes interrupted, and although rape is almost impossible to predict and to avoid with certainty, women dedicate enormous amounts of time changing their behaviour in order to "prevent/avoid/limit it in their lives" to use Liz Kelley's formulation.

Most rape research globally suggests that women are more likely to be raped by men they know than to be abducted in public by men they may not know, or men they may not know well. This literature is often held up to debunk the notion of rapists as strangers. Feminists do not argue that nobody is ever raped by a stranger, only that these cases are the exception rather than the rule.

This is something that is very often taken for granted as a given, and the experience of service providers for survivors very often support this. However, in the South African situation, there is a case to be made for patterns of public abductions of women by men they do not have a relationship with. While women sometimes recognised the faces of the men attempting to/abducting them in the jackrolling in what was then the Transvaal or other gang-rape abductions in the Cape Town townships or Durban concerts in the 1980s and 1990s, this recognition was often because some of these men were notorious serial rapists. To recognise the faces of certain men because you have witnessed them abduct women in public before is not the same as knowing these men. For all intents and purposes, these men are strangers.

The same can be said of the practice of ukuthwala, which although not new, seems to have gained prominence in some rural areas of the Eastern Cape and KwaZulu-Natal. The men who abduct young women, sometimes children, are not always known to the women they attack. And, since abducted women for purposes of forced marriage are often raped before payment is exchanged as *lobola*, this site presents another instance of strangers abducting/ attacking women in public. I am not referring to those instances of staged ukuthwala where lovers agree to this beforehand in order to force their families to agree to an otherwise resisted marriage.

I raise these two types of abductions partly because of the generation of South African women I belong to and because I remember how much time my peers spent discussing the fear of being jackrolled or being accosted by iintsara when they went back home for the holidays from boarding school, as well as very vivid recollections of loved ones whose bodies friends held onto in resistance when a notorious gangster sought to abduct them. In my early teens, I also recall the sudden obsessive watchfulness of my mother towards me and my sisters when we visited Nkgono in rural Matatiele, as well as the anxious whisperings when girls whose breasts had just barely sprouted were being abducted by men from neighbouring villages who wanted to turn them into wives.

The female fear factory, and the fear of gendered violence in public spaces is therefore not simply symbolic. It is also part of the recent experience of growing up as a woman in South Africa and witnessing young women your age disappear and return, if at all, with broken spirits. This is a significant part of the collective unspoken, and it requires that we temper our allocation of stranger rape to the margins of our anti-rape work. While it may not be a significant part of how most women experience rape today in South Africa, it is a large part of the narrative of rape for those of us who were teenagers in the eighties and early nineties.

Public threats of violence against women, and widespread sexual harassment in public places are part of how women are rendered fearful because the manufacture of female fear is a public phenomenon. In a recent conversation, I was asked how attitudes of men can be changed in relation to different dimensions of gendered violence. Most people in the conversation argued that education about the real harm and prevalence of violence against women would go a long way. I am not convinced that this kind of education works. Given the fact that the female fear factory as well as the specific manifestations of public abduction for rape I discuss above happened openly, and were witnessed by different genders, I am not sure why men from these spaces would need education. Surely men who walk the streets hear women sexually harassed, turn away from threats of rape issued around them, and are therefore part of the same factory women are pulled into.

Increasingly, and along with Beth Quinn, I suspect that:

> gender differences in interpreting [gender based violence] stem not so much from men's not getting it. [...] but from a studied, often compulsory, lack of motivation to identify with women's experiences.... Men learn that to effectively perform masculine identity, they must, in many instances, ignore a woman's pain and obscure her viewpoint.

The averted gaze is implicated in this choice to ignore, as we saw in the story involving Lebo Pule earlier in this chapter. The young man's response to the woman who resisted his advances understood her intention but chose not to value it. This is because, as Quinn notes again:

Sexually [violent] behaviors are produced from more than a lack of knowledge, simple sexist attitudes, or misplaced sexual desire. Some ... are mechanisms through which gendered boundaries are patrolled and evoked and by which deeply held identities are established.

I am often surprised by the ability of some men and women who publicly opposed gendered violence to mutate and speak differently when away from the public glare. Gender-based violence discourse in South Africa is both very loud, in important ways, and very dangerous.

Walking out of a radio discussion on Kaya fm once, a man who represented a men's organisation that teaches men to unlearn violence against women, who had minutes before shared the work they do with men to help them unlearn patriarchal entitlement to women's and girls' bodies, turned to me in the parking lot and tried to entangle me in a conversation about how some forms of rape are understandable (between lovers) but that the rest of it needs to be fought because it is brutality. I would name the organisation if I still remembered its name, but since it was not one whose work I had been familiar with prior to the interview, I now battle to recall it.

I have lost count of how many times I have fought with, or heard of another person fighting with, a scholar of masculinities who says that men have a crisis. Two years ago, at a meeting about sexual harassment at the institution that pays me, several male colleagues bemoaned the manner in which they feel unsure and under attack, don't know whether to leave their doors open, how to talk to women students who so often come on to them, but they don't want to tarnish their careers. This is part of the backlash because we are now required to make them feel better about being men in the world in ways that ensure we stop talking about what is under discussion: the routine violation of women because we are women.

CHAPTER 5

Making sense of responses to the Jacob Zuma rape trial

As I put the final touches to this book, it has been nine years since the Jacob Zuma rape trial. One very brave and incisive book *The Kanga and the Kangaroo Court: the Trial of Jacob Zuma*, written by Mmatshilo Motsei is the only book on the topic. I know of two manuscripts on the trial whose publication has been thwarted, although I hope that this will prove to have been a long delay. The trial inspired and provoked an outpouring of writing in creative, op-ed, journalist and academic publications. The range of perspectives explored in this material tells us something about the perceived importance of this trial. It was a difficult moment in South Africa's post-transition period and one that questioned many assumptions about the place of power, gender and sexuality in our society. The trial took place as much inside the walls of the court as it did in the court of public opinion, a space that included the kangaroo-style courts that Motsei addresses.

Whereas rape has long been a preoccupation of post-apartheid South African public talk, the trial revealed great chasms in how different South Africans understand rape, and choose to respond to someone accused of rape, on the one hand, and a woman who laid a charge of rape, on the other. The positions that people – as individuals and groups – took in relation to the trial also spilled over into other areas of private and public life. In this chapter, I am concerned with some public responses to the Zuma trial. It is not an attempt to map what all the public responses were. It will take a lot more research by many more people for us to be able to engage in such a cartographic exercise. Cartography – map-making – like plotting along a line also makes things much tidier than they really are. It makes things appear much simpler, yet responses to rape are not simple and tidy, as the trial highlighted.

This trial at the end of which Jacob Zuma was acquitted of raping the woman we know as Khwezi, was a significant moment in the history of South Africa's relationships with rape. It was a mere six months from media reports of Khwezi's rape charge and 8 May 2006, the date on which Judge Willem van der Merwe found Jacob Zuma not guilty of rape, rebuked Khwezi for 'lying' to the court and criticised Zuma for recklessly 'having sex' with Khwezi. Much that transpired inside and outside the court was instructive of how we deal with rape, why rape survivors make certain choices, and the fraught ways in which the legal system responds to and treats rape complainants. What was simultaneously brought into focus was why we are losing the battle against rape, risk aspects of the HIV/ AIDS pandemic that often seem puzzling from macro-analyses, as well as contested ideas about women's bodies and people's sexual orientations. What was surfaced in the trial also intersects with all of the issues explored in the other chapters of this book. The trial also provoked many more questions than it answered about public valuations and responses to charges of rape.

At the end of 2005, the *Sunday Times* broke the story that a charge of rape had been laid against then Deputy President Jacob Gedleyihlekisa Zuma; several other newspapers also picked this up. The charges were laid by a young woman, a well-known HIV-positive activist, lesbian daughter of Zuma's late comrade. The 31-year-old woman reported that Zuma, whom she had previously related to as a father-figure or uncle, raped her in his Forest Town home on 3 November 2005. These media reports were met with various denials by those who represented Zuma. Confronted with repeated denials, the Afrikaans newspaper, *Beeld* first published the Hillbrow police station case number, and later revealed the complainant's identity. On the face of it, the publication of Khwezi's name was an attempt to prove that such a charge had been laid against Zuma. It was to function as evidence for what some papers had already reported on, and since this was a serious charge against an important public figure, the news had public value. This was not the only effect of such publication, however. South African law says a rape complainant may not be named, and this is with a view to protecting her privacy and also mindful of the enormous stigma that continues to attach itself to survivors of rape. When the newspaper published the complainant's name, it was in flagrant disregard for her right to privacy. Here, the importance of being right mattered more than the unethical exposure of the woman who had laid the charge. This incident set the stage and pace for the media's central role in the unfolding of the drama that was to lead to Zuma's acquittal at the end of the trial. This move was to set the tone for the public contestations that were to characterise everything associated with the trial.

While the staff of the newspaper could not have predicted what was to unfold, the media was the way in which the vast majority of the public accessed news about the trial. While thousands turned out daily in a show of unprecedented support outside court post-apartheid, millions more relied on what the radio, television and newspapers reported as important about the trial.

As the publication of the complainant's name shows, this was a case that was important and proved to be a watershed moment for what it highlighted about societal attitudes that had previously been slightly out of view. The euphoria of a new country with progressive legislation and a groundbreaking Bill of Rights were the pride of the New South Africa. Yet, by 2005 it was equally clear that there was a disjuncture between the values of the Constitution and the behaviour of the populace. Rape statistics were – and continue to be – alarmingly high. Newspapers were saturated with reports of contradictory attitudes to rape: low rates of successful prosecution, the very slow pace of the legal process, low sentences handed down, worrisome reports of the criminal justice system, secondary victimisation by the police and inside courts, public derision of women who spoke out against rape, including by the judge who castigated women's organisations' interest in the case as based on agendas and 'prejudging' the facts of the case, and defensiveness about the mere mention of rape. All of these came to most people through media reportage. So, the media's role is very important in reflecting on and shaping public perception.

The media played no different a role in the rape case of Jacob Zuma. Across the spectrum, the media staged responses that ranged from disbelief and confusion, on the one hand, to rage and support, on the other. It was a case that split South Africans in very stark ways and revealed daily the vast chasms in values and perceptions among South African residents, demonstrating how powerful these differences were on how gender and sexuality matter. While the 'rainbow nation' and 'united in diversity' motifs had long been questioned, until this trial, race and class investments had been assumed to be the dominant fault lines.

To speak about the media's role is also somewhat misleading since reportage and contestation took on varied expression across the media landscape. And, although opinion is explicitly staged on the analysis and editorial pages with the journalistic sections of the paper often described as 'impartial', this case more than any other showed the fallacy of this insistence on journalistic neutrality. This is not a new matter. Many consumers and media audiences understand that neutrality is a myth and make decisions on which outlets to tune into, call or write into or buy accordingly.

So how did the media speak about the trial and what did these choices reveal about South African society and attitudes? Theses could be written on answering that question alone. But there are ways in which we can answer the question, even if partially, and my choices for this chapter are limited to three national weekend newspapers: *City Press, Mail and Guardian* and *Sunday Times*. I choose these for their reach, and recognise that looking at radio, television, newspapers in a different language, regional publications, magazines rather than newspapers, tabloids rather than broadsheet, and so forth, would reveal different parts of the pie that is South African public opinion. Nonetheless, looking at these three large newspapers, which boasted circulation numbers of 187 741, 43 050, and 504 301, respectively between April and June 2006 allows entry into broad societal attitudes to all the issues associated with the rape trial that I am particularly interested in here. These newspapers show stances taken by national media and give us entry into circulating values and understandings of rape in our society.

Second, and equally important to point out, for the purposes of this chapter I am less interested in the accused Jacob Zuma as a person vis à vis the trial. What is instructive about the trial is how ordinary it was, as various feminist writers such as Pregs Govender, Nikki Naylor, Vanessa Ludwig and I pointed out in our public writing at the time. To the extent that the trial held a magnifying glass – or mirror as Shireen Hassim argues – on a typical rape case by allowing its various dimensions to be played out in the public glare of the media, we are able to examine some ways in which rape is imagined, understood and explained by groups of South Africans, and therefore perhaps better continue to reflect on strategies against it. It is also important to identify the ways in which the trial was not typical. The exceptions identified by Lisa Vetten and Liesl Gerntholtz included:

First, the swiftness with which the case was wrapped up, a period of less than a year from laying a charge to verdict, whereas usually "complainants wait for years before their cases come to court".

Second, Khwezi's placement in witness protection which "is not usually extended to rape survivors in less high profile cases, and many women face threats and intimidation from perpetrators and their family and friends".

Third, the proper collection and presentation of DNA evidence to the court, whereas "in many cases, the evidence is not collected at the scene of the rape, or is lost, or is never presented to the court due to an enormous backlog at the forensic laboratory that delays much forensic analysis."

Added to these differences was the spotlight on various aspects of the case and the ways in which many actors not directly involved in the legal proceedings could partake in its analysis. In other words, what callers into radio shows said, what letters ordinary people wrote into various print outlets argued, what journalists chose to highlight, interpret, anticipate and/or edit out, all offered a rare window into how South Africa thinks about rape, sexuality and power. This is what Hassim points to when she writes about the trial holding a mirror to South Africa. All of these ideas and interpretations existed prior to Khwezi laying a charge of rape, and they are directly implicated in our inability to curb the frequency of rape in South Africa.

Fourth, while the media does not simply reflect societal dynamics back for that same society's consumption, media choices about representation, what to highlight, what to omit and so forth are connected to how gendered and other identities are negotiated in the society such media both addresses and forms a part of. Observing the media coverage, it is clear there was a certain idiom that emerged during the few months that Jacob Zuma was on trial for rape. Media scholar David Gauntlett asks whether in fact the most important debate about "the social impact of the media" isn't "does the mass media have a significant amount of power over its audience, or does the audience ultimately have more power than the media?"

There are numerous approaches to analysing media, as scholars of media – whether of journalism, communication, audiences, cultural studies, or political economy of the media – know. I am not concerned with the media in and as of itself, here, but with how these newspapers function as a public staging of certain contestations. The moments staged in the media tell us about various processes that influenced the heightened public contestation

105

around the trial. In other words, what does the mirror Hassim speaks of show, where and how? This is why I am interested in a variety of spaces within the newspapers I choose, and spaces that use different kinds of registers. Because of this, in my quest to answer the questions of what the media revealed about the trial and our society's relationships to rape, news items, letters and analysis pages all matter.

All of these very different kinds of writing provide us with a barometer of sorts into dimensions of the collective psyche of audiences constituted by these newspapers. The letters pages of all three newspapers were abuzz, as were the letters pages of many other regional newspapers that are not analysed in this chapter. This heightened activity and increased determination – perhaps passion – to write into the newspapers is a small indicator of many people's feelings about the importance of the case. This is largely because most newspaper readers do not routinely write to the editors, nor do all of those who write get published on the pages designated for such correspondence.

Fifth, never before has the public sphere been so visibly taken to by feminist commentators and repeatedly on the same media outlets that they sometimes took issue with. Some of this writing came at great cost – personal and financial. Some commentators had work contracts cancelled and calls unreturned when they suddenly found themselves on opposing sides of the rape trial divide from colleagues, or when their public opinions were seen to threaten future finances for employers. Friendships were terminated, longstanding relationships were also threatened and sometimes irreparably damaged as partners or friends woke up to positions on the case that were not only diametrically opposed but offensive to each other. When one partner believes the complainant and argues that those who vocally support the accused are not only trivialising rape but guilty of secondary victimisation, on the one hand, and the second partner believes that the accused is either being maligned or singled out as part of a conspiracy since he is not the only one guilty of such an offence, on the other, repercussions may be felt in other aspects of the relationship. Nor was this cost only to feminist commentators.

Given the politics of access to publishing in mainstream media in South Africa, I am aware that chances are that many more feminist submissions, letters and other opinion and analysis pieces were submitted than were published. Still, the significant volumes and high visibility of feminist commentary and overall explicit engagement with the media by readers was notable.

Writing letters, opinion pieces and other analysis for the newspapers was not the only feminist intervention. The most significant came from the women's groups that came together to form the One in Nine Campaign, to provide various forms of support for the woman they called Khwezi during the trial. Although One in Nine Campaign could not have anticipated the tens of thousands of people who came to support the accused during the trial, most of the pioneer group were seasoned activists in the fight against gendered violence. Many of them had extensive experience of supporting rape complainants through the system, were trained counsellors, were well versed in the legal justice system, and many were themselves survivors of sexual violence. They had high visibility as the purple T-shirt-clad women inside and outside court. They had to brave harassment and threats as they did so. Women in purple T-shirts protested outside and inside the court in support of the complainant, whom they had named Khwezi, since complainants in rape cases cannot be named unless they make decisions to the contrary. They had chosen to call her Khwezi, fully aware of the earlier breach by the newspaper to rebuff Zuma's denial that a charge of rape had been laid against him. Feminist interventions also included the application for *amici curiae* – friends of the court – a strategy that was hotly debated and critiqued inside and outside feminist communities, and the various public and academic responses offered as critique, intervention and response to the trial.

Who, then, was the Zuma of the South African national media?

Under a headline "She isn't my daughter" published in the *Mail and Guardian* of 31 March–6 April, 2006, Fikile-Ntsikelelo Moya writes a speculative piece that attempts to predict what Zuma will do and say in court the following week as he takes the witness stand. The narrative, then, centres Zuma, and lists a series of 'expectations', the basis of which is left unexplored. In this piece, Moya mentions the complainant only in passing as illustration for what Zuma is expected to say. The expectations are based on how Zuma could frame a defence:

> Zuma will have to convince the court that his relationship with the alleged rape victim was not that of a father to a daughter. [...] He is expected [to] point to the infrequency of their contact in between the return from exile and the night of the alleged rape. [...] He is also expected to testify on why no criminal intent should be inferred from the cellphone conversation and the flurry of SMS messages [sic] he exchanged with the complainant, her mother, family friend Zweli Mkhize and others after the alleged rape. [...] Zuma's effort will not only be an effort to clear his name, but to give a watching nation a sense that the case is complete.

Moya can reliably predict that Zuma's defence will resemble the defence in many rape cases, which is not that no sexual contact occurred, but rather that it was consensual, not violation. To engage in the speculative exercise, Moya has to read the case as an ordinary rape case, with the predictable, familiar defence. In order to stand a chance of acquittal, an accused in a rape case would have to make consensual sex believable, and in this case, would have to remove the suggestion that they have a relationship of parent and child or uncle and niece. Removal of this kind of family association allows the defendant to frame consensual sex as not just possible but also acceptable, whereas sex with his daughter or niece would transgress acceptable standards of morality and therefore backfire for the accused. Moya infers that success at these two moves creates plausibility since it increases the possibility of the court believing the accused that no crime had been committed. However, to be completely believable, Zuma would have to also explain the flurry of messages between the parties named, given the infrequent contact prior to the contested night.

Moya does not clarify whose expectations he lists, but he need not. They are probably informed by some legal opinion. Furthermore, Moya shows in his predictions and the authority invested in these expectations through the use of the passive voice with no identifiable actor, that the case will follow a predictable rape case script. This is a script that is familiar to many readers even if they have no actual firsthand experience of a rape court case. Part of this familiarity is through the media, largely television legal dramas both locally made and from elsewhere, a very popular genre. Moya thus positions himself and the reader as co-knowers of what is expected to transpire the following week. However, if the content of the article is already shared – or common knowledge – then its detailing here is redundant, unless we recognise that rhetorically it works less as a source of information and more as a way of constituting shared community with his readers. Shared background knowledge, assumptions and expectation reinforce the reader's connection to Moya. Alternatively, the reader, who does not feel constituted as insider and therefore does not recognise the knowledge presented by Moya, is cast in the position of outsider allowed entry and access to valuable knowledge. This impression is buttressed by the news item placed immediately below Moya's piece, one that attempts to demonstrate *vox pop*.

The item uses a question as title, "Is JZ still the worker's darling?" and is subtitled "a straw poll by Monako Dibetle indicates that Zuma remains a firm favourite of the person in the street". The four people interviewed all offer unconditional support for Zuma.

The two news items intersect in interesting ways. The first does not quote Zuma as suggested but rather refers to what he is expected to say. In fact, Zuma does not speak at all in the article. The second headline is revealing; the use of 'still' requires shared prior knowledge of this as once true. Unlike Moya's piece where Zuma appears as the archetypal accused expected to perform exceedingly well in the rape script known to all, in the second, he is intimately familiar: beloved. The straw poll confirms that the accused continues to be the worker's darling. The larger suggestion is that the rape has changed little for him outside the court.

Whereas Moya's piece sets out a script that needs to be performed well, Dibetle's poll shows that he need not perform at all in the court of public opinion. His position as the 'darling' of the workers is secure. The inference to be made is that the case is a minor glitch which has not changed much of how people perceive or feel about Zuma. The language of affection is also one of loyalty through trying times. It is a language of intimate access and knowledge of the person; however, the sources' intimate loyalty is for a man there is no evidence they know personally.

Loyalty, unlike the rape defence script, does not depend on his actions. It remains regardless of actions. However, Zuma is able to abdicate responsibility because loyalty is not dependent on his actions. Furthermore, if he is popular with 'ordinary people', who does that make those critical of him, and even more disturbingly, his accuser?

Loyalty requires the unforgivable to rupture, and clearly for security guard Morris Mabaso, South African Transport and Allied Workers Union (SATAWU) member, rape is not unforgivable, since he notes "Whether guilty or innocent, we still want him as our leader because he is a good man." In the same vein, Mamorena Moloi, South African Clothing and Textile Workers Union (SACTWU) member is concerned about Zuma contracting HIV but is quite confident that consensual sex occurred and that the rape charge is fabricated. She ends "I don't care about the girl ... We want him as our leader, but why did he sleep with an infected person, knowing she is infected?" For taxi driver Lucky Ngwenya, also a SATAWU member, Zuma's good character is self-evident, even from a distance. Ngwenya ends "[y]ou hear by the way he addresses him that he's a good man." The final person quoted, Thandi Dimba, member of the National Education and Health Workers Union (NEHAWU), has travelled from Durban to "support Zuma", and she, like Mabaso, finds it irrelevant whether in fact Zuma is guilty or not as she confidently declares, first, "we will continue supporting him, guilty or not" and then, even more revealingly, "[w]e, as women, need to respect ourselves and our bodies. We need to stand up for the truth and not support chancers that are against Zuma."

For all of the workers interviewed, the facts of the case are irrelevant. Rape does not matter. What does matter are their feelings for Zuma. Unlike the previous article on the same page, where Zuma needs to perform successfully in order to stand a chance at acquittal, for the workers interviewed, the court room is a side show. It is the court of public opinion that matters, and there, Zuma comes out on top. What is striking is the repetition of the insignificance of rape, as well as the insignificance of the complainant. Perhaps the latter is explained by Dima's parting shot that places the burden of safety from rape on women. Here, she cites a different, but familiar script that holds that women can escape rape if they assume appropriate femininity. In other words, for Dima, Khwezi only needed to behave properly, to "respect herself and her body" in order to escape rape. The language and logic used by Dima here is of slut-shaming, and one that sees women as solely responsible for how men treat them. It is Khwezi who needs shaming, Dima suggests, because women who do not respect themselves are liars, and unreliable and need to be opposed by women like Dima who are their opposites. Slut-shaming is the phenomenon of casting aspersions on a person's sexual behaviour as inappropriate and undesirable through marking it as shameful. Here Dima reads Khwezi as a liar who had inappropriate sex, or put herself in danger of rape by behaving inappropriately.

On the same page, up against the far-right edge, in a single column, is Liesl Gerntholtz's commentary on why the contentious *amici curiae* application matters. Gerntholtz explains the relevance of the intervention by a group that sought status as *amici curiae* to the High Court, a group composed of the Centre for the Study of Violence and Reconciliation, the Centre for Applied Legal Studies, and Tshwaranang Legal Advocacy Centre, all groups with a significant presence in women's rights work. She explains that the three groups were motivated by the desire to assist the court "on important issues that the court needs to decide during legal proceedings", that they had been motivated by a history of successfully acting in this capacity on matters to do with reproductive rights, HIV/AIDS and freedom of expression, underlining also that this "particular type of *amicus* has been used effectively by many civil society organisations." Finally, although the judge rejected the application, Gerntholtz optimistically muses about the advantages of "enter[ing] the fray" outweighing the disadvantages and her hope that it "will send a clear message of support and encouragement to other rape survivors." The decision of the group to apply for *amicus* drew from experiences within the Criminal Justice System and specific kinds of cases where women were disadvantaged due to court officials' blind spots. Being accepted as *amici curiae* enables the court to access expert and background information on the matter at hand that is not necessarily part of the court proceedings. It has a long record of successful application by civil society to get more just outcomes for the participants in a court case.

What Gerntholtz's optimism points to is this background as well as the publicity that was generated by the controversial decision taken by these organisations to apply to be admitted as *amici curiae* against the will of the complainant.

The disadvantages Gerntholtz refers to stem from the fact that Khwezi disagreed with the application and had outright rejected the tactic and the attempt to assist her in this particular way. Consequently, the application was highly criticised by the feminists who supported Khwezi and had formed the One in Nine Campaign, and who wore purple T-shirts inside and outside the court. On the whole, feminists in South Africa disagreed significantly on the validity of the move. On the one hand, the applicants pointed to the manner in which courts often did not take matters of gender rights with due attention to the details and how women who appeared before the court were frequently disadvantaged by the court's 'gender blindness', which really translated to gender-insensitivity. On the other hand, were feminists who agreed with this group on the courts' record of gender-insensitivity but argued that the feminist principle of respecting what a survivor wanted to do about her rape was paramount. The disagreement was not a polite one, but one that also fed deep suspiciousness between different strands of feminist movements within South Africa.

It did not help matters that the applicants were predominantly white feminists, while those who opposed the application were predominantly Black. Contestations, tensions and wounds between Black feminists and white feminists, as groups, run deep in South Africa in ways that resonate globally. The disadvantages, then, included widening a rift that many had worked hard to address and narrow. At the same time, it is important to note that this was not a tidy disagreement between liberal white feminists, on one side, and anti-racist Black feminists, on the other, although some of the discussions echoed this older disagreement and pain. In fact, there were anti-racist feminists on both sides. Both sides were populated by feminists with deep roots in feminist activist work, and there were many longstanding traditions of working collectively across this divide. In other words, it is important to remember the distinction between being a feminist who is white/ Black and the ideological sites within feminism that go under the rubric of white/Black feminism.

This *Mail and Guardian* page seems to have juxtaposed very different approaches to the Zuma rape trial: those who recognised that the case had all the characteristics of a typical rape case and would be predictable in some of the proceedings of the court, represented here by Moya's article. Second, were those who would support Zuma unconditionally and cared little for the formal proceedings within the court. Their loyalty knew no bounds and nothing would dissuade them in this support as well as their disapproval – and sometimes disdain – for Khwezi. For the second group, what mattered was the court of public opinion and as tens of thousands travelled to support Zuma outside court, it became clear just how organised this group was. Third, were those who sought to support Khwezi in a variety of ways successful and otherwise.

The union members come from three of the Congress of South African Trade Union's (COSATU's) then twenty-one affiliates, one of the alliance members with the African National Congress and the South African Communist Party (SACP). They not only speak as workers and 'ordinary people', but they also speak from the official left. This newspaper's approach on this page is cartographic: an attempt to map public sentiment, trends and patterns. Throughout the case, the *Mail and Guardian* layout choices remained interesting. So are many of its headline choices on positioning, especially news coverage. Later headlines, such as "In defence of Kemp J Kemp" led readers to ask why Zuma's lawyer needs defending, against whom and what, questions that were not adequately addressed in the body of the article. Such headlines also buttress the wildly circulating accusations that Zuma was a victim of a political conspiracy.

Despite its stated *vox pop*, the same paper also published letters to the editor that showed that the public was very divided on Zuma; the pages of the paper became contested space since the editorial, comments and analysis and letters to the editor's pages showed more differentiated views than suggested by the headlines and news items.

I have spent considerable time on one edition, mainly because it was representative of this paper's coverage of the trial. I will return to some of the commentary that appeared in the Comments and Analysis pages later in the chapter.

City Press pages were also contested terrain, but they revealed a different set of investments in reporting and reflecting on the case. Seven of the eleven letters published in the 16 April edition responded specifically to the previous week's column by Redi Direko in which she had sharply criticised Zuma's behaviour inside and outside court. Mkhululi Kobe from Port Elizabeth prefaced his letter with the admission that the Zuma trial had so significantly polarised society that he had been warned to hold his tongue in order to better safeguard his future economic and professional ambitions. His letter notes an example of the kind of personal and financial costs that often stemmed from positions individuals took vis à vis the Jacob Zuma rape trial. In order to be safe, he was being warned to hold his tongue since he had nothing to lose if nobody knows where he stands. He cannot be disadvantaged in career and finances if those in a position to benefit him in monetary terms or advance his career do not know his stance on the trial, which may very well run contrary to theirs. The fact that Kobe mentions this advice, only to then publicly ignore it signals that he thinks what is at stake is quite significant.

Kobe chooses to point out Zuma's contradictory allusion to Zulu culture by noting how many understood norms he discards at will, including compromising his own daughter's integrity by making her speak on her father's sexuality. He ends with, "[t]he final judgment in court will not change the moral judgment society has passed on Zuma." For Kobe, Zuma has behaved inappropriately and he will deal with these consequences regardless of the outcome of the court case. If Zuma really holds Zulu cultural norms in high regard as he claims, he should be consistent and keep his child out of his sexual matters, according to Kobe. Zuma has failed to keep the required distance between his relationship with his children and his sexual activities, and therefore only alludes to Zulu cultural values when this will advance his case, flouting them when doing so will serve him well. It is therefore a consistency and moral parenting test Zuma fails in Kobe's eyes that will cost him in future.

Reporting on the fact that the complainant had relocated after the trial, Wonder Hlongwa and S'thembiso Msomi write under the headline "'Unsafe' JZ accuser relocated" on 16 April. Prior to this the media had reported widely on threats to the complainant and her family, outside the court, attacks on the homes of her family members, and the burning of her photocopied pictures. The placing of 'unsafe' under question is interesting against this backdrop. The effect of this questioning of her safety is to render her unreliable, and undermine the credibility of those who have reported on threats to Khwezi's life. The effect is that the complainant's word is once again posed against Zuma and 'the public'. It matters little that her unsafety has been variously corroborated, or that many Zuma supporters outside court openly threatened her.

Other articles (co)written for the newspaper by Msomi were equally interesting in how they positioned Zuma and Khwezi. Two items from the 2 April issue, "Can JZ bail himself out?" and "Day of reckoning in the dock for Msholozi", and "Sika lekhekhe, sika lekhekhe!" of 16 April are particularly revealing.

The casualness and affection in "JZ" echoing the 'cool masculinity' of a rap star similarly named, but also on its own a shorterning coupled with the playful connotations of bailing himself out, make light of the very serious charges he is facing. The second headline from the same day is reliant on equally affectionate terms, softening the biblical judgment-day rhetoric with reference to Zuma by his clan name, thereby creating a space of immediacy. The content of the articles are consistent with what the headlines signal.

What is more, Msomi's headlines from the 16 April issue refer jointly to the literal cutting and sharing of cakes celebrating Zuma's birthday while the trial continued and the general festive mood which sat oddly with what was transpiring inside the court. In a disturbing and deliberate confluence of meanings, however, *City Press* readers know that Msomi's article is headlined with an intertextual reference to kwaito musician, Arthur Mafokate's hit song of the same name.

Mafokate's crude song relies on hegemonic references to vaginas as cake to be consumed, cutting it then for precisely this. Additionally, Mafokate habitually sexually objectifies both adult women and girl dancers in his videos and live performances. In other words, Mafokate's register is often both hypersexual and pornographic. The parallels between the sexual/sexual-violence performances in the public domain would be evident to readers, which is why they are appealed to here.

Later, *City Press* was to publish divergent opinions by two members of its editorial staff on the *amici curiae* application: Mathatha Tsedu and Gail Smith (2 and 9 April respectively). However, with the exception of Redi Direko's comment on 9 April, which led to a huge response in the letters pages the following week, and Smith's article, *City Press* coverage was clearly biased towards casting Jacob Zuma in as favourable a light as possible.

The pages of the *Sunday Times* showed consistent contestation for the duration of the trial. Its editor wrote a very strongly worded critique of Zuma's ethnicist posturing and appeal to colonialist masculinity at the same time as offering extensive space for critique of Zuma's gender politics by other prominent Black male activists and intellectuals.

Charles Molele, Moipone Malefane and Ndivhuho Mafela's article on how Zuma's supporters responded to the prosecutor also invited critical engagement with the events of the trial by questioning the basis of the attacks: "Supporters lambaste 'impertinent' prosecutor" was the chosen headline for their 9 April story. This contributed to reader Ben Mokoena's complaint that the paper and its editor were "hellbent on destroying Zuma" in his letter published on 16 April.

Interestingly, the *Sunday Times* coverage offered a critical stance on Zuma as a whole, although it is noteworthy that, as with the first two newspapers analysed above, the focus was predominantly on Zuma as the (more) important actor in the public imagination. This was as true of the romanticisation evident in Msomi (*City Press*) and Moya (*Mail and Guardian*) in characterising Zuma vis à vis the trial and the South African populace on the one hand, as it was in the more critical approach adopted in most *Sunday Times* news items.

From the above begins to emerge a sense of who the media's Zuma is, even if it is not a clear-cut, tidy and complete image. The media's Zuma is the central protagonist and part of the trial: he is the hero or anti-hero of the trial/narrative. In other words, the trial is about him most importantly.

Secondly, the media's Zuma is susceptible to the law, which is fair and should have the final say on the matter. Thirdly, he is a Zulu man who can use this location to explain himself although this can be contested. Finally, sex and sexuality are complicated and Zuma can demonstrate some degree of folly.

The comments and analysis pages of all three newspapers also reflected the contestation over the meanings of the Jacob Zuma trial. Some of the disagreements also directly addressed earlier material published as analysis. On the pages of *City Press*, Gail Smith disagreed with the stance adopted by Mathatha Tsedu, her editor, on the *amicus curiae* application. Tsedu's piece argued that the decision to disregard Khwezi's wishes was callous and deserving of contempt since it sought to take power away from someone already disempowered by the spectacle outside court and the difficult proceedings inside the court. Smith insisted that the applicants were justified and that "South Africa needs more interfering busybodies like these." Part of the argument Smith was making was that violence was not a personal matter, and that part of recognising it as political required a multi-layered approach worth the risk.

Sibongile Ndashe's critique on the rape trial also pertained to the ways in which public discussion sought to silence support for both Khwezi specifically, and rape complainants in general. She wrote:

> This distraction is quintessential of sidetracking that forces black women to engage in fringe issues, whilst attempts are made to silence our voices. [...] The password is often a demand for qualifiers that have become a pre-requisite for debate on gender based violence. So one needs to say 'not all men are rapists, and that in the past some people have been falsely accused'. Having said that, I would have unlocked my audience.

This gate-keeping and requirement of passwords was exhausting and a silencing strategy that needed to be met with contempt, as Ndashe showed. It was a sidetracking manoeuvre and an attempt to determine the terms of discussion in patriarchal ways.

By and large, feminist analyses published in these newspapers as well as other media outlets seemed to work from a different set of starting points and assumptions, as Smith and Ndashe above have started to show. For starters, they did not move from the assumption that Zuma was innocent until an impartial legal process showed otherwise. Aware of how disadvantaged rape complainants are in the Criminal Justice System, they paid attention to the details of the case and also insisted that what happened outside the court mattered.

For the purposes of expediency, feminist responses will be seen as those that were offered by critics who self-identify as feminist framed their public interventions as such, and those responses that rely on feminist conceptual tools by critiquing patriarchal logic to engage with the trial where the writer's self-identification was unclear. Feminists worked from a different starting point on the trial and did so unapologetically. Many expressed dismay at the failure of the criminal justice system, but were at pains to point out that they were not surprised by this since it is an institution that was consistently hostile to women. Many of us brought our experience of dealing with rape complainants and doing other anti-patriarchal work to bear on our analyses of how the state treated Khwezi.

Writing in *Pambazuka,* Vanessa Ludwig, Sibongile Ndashe and Nikki Naylor problematised aspects of the legal system and case. Ludwig noted that the verdict on the Zuma rape case, although expected, showed that the legal system "has been found guilty of being hostile to women, Black women in particular; it is guilty of its refusal to protect us." The trial had been predictable but there had been clear ways in which Khwezi has been disregarded, such as the way she spoke about her identity as lesbian, which was dismissed and replaced by another marker of identity as bisexual. How then was a system that would not even allow a woman to choose what to call herself be trusted to protect her and offer her the possibility of justice?

Feminist lawyers Ndashe and Naylor treated legal instruments with suspicion, insisting that women not be fooled by patriarchal institutions that claimed impartiality. This analysis was extended to specific manifestations of family as well. Naylor wrote that one of the effects of the case was the over-simplistic reliance on court cases and the legal system to correct what are, in effect, far-reaching social incompetencies. They problematised the court's treatment and inclusion of Khwezi's sexual past and sexual-violence history, arguing that part of what the procedure communicated to women who had a past, and therefore all women, was that it makes no sense for women to report rape since there is no realistic chance that the average woman, who lives an interesting, dynamic life, and asserts sexual agency in terms of play, intercourse or any other expression, can attain justice. Naylor continued to grapple with how to claim agency, go for counselling and still retain feminist arguments for sexual play and ambiguity, when the mere presence of a sexual history – consensual and forced – will continue to be the primary tool in re-victimisation of those who report rape. After this trial, clearly the average woman could "never be able to place [herself] in a witness box" with confidence. Yet, Naylor's exasperation was tempered with the knowledge that, as feminists we need to continue to "add [our voices] in the name of the movement for other women to speak out."

Writing about the urgent need to find new ways of doing feminist work against rape, Naylor reflected on our collective defeat when faced with the specific tenor of the trial inside and outside court, writing wishfully, "[m]ay this silence be akin to the quiet before the storm. And that when we break it, nothing but thunderbolts of new voices should leave our mouths," whereas, coming from the same sense of frustration, I wrote in the *Mail and Guardian* of the urgency of crafting those new tools in order to be better able "to defend ourselves against the status quo [misogynists] uphold, and against them."

One of the most striking features of many of the feminist-written pieces was the insistence by many who entered the space that they believed Khwezi, thereby positioning themselves as very separate from those who had placed the burden of proof on her and presumed Zuma innocent. Pregs Govender called Khwezi "a rape survivor [who] exercised her right to charge her alleged perpetrator, a very powerful man", Barney Pityana called her the "complainant/victim/survivor", Ndashe called all men who testified to having "sex" with her as a child and an adult a "gang", the statement by 54 African women declared that they "publicly state that we stand in solidarity with Khwezi ... she has our love and support." In this intervention, she was not an incurable and opportunistic liar. Nor was she damaged and in need of special counselling because of psychological damage, as many argued.

Second, feminist interventions focused on Khwezi. They either addressed themselves to her specifically, claimed alliance with her through sharing her pain as one they deemed unfairly treated, subjected to secondary rape and other forms of violence at the trial, all of which is evident in writing by Gasa, Govender, Gqola, Nkutha and Pityana. Unlike the alleged impartial and fact-based reporting and support of Zuma which relied on institutional buttressing, feminist commentary embraced the world of emotion. Redi Direko's rage rose defiantly off the page, but was also elegantly owned in her piece, Pityana's sadness and Gasa's pain were equally owned. Linking the pain that responsible, humane individuals should experience upon being forced to witness a woman's violation being turned into what Govender called a "pornographic feeding frenzy", Pityana was taken aback by Zuma and his camp's lack of shame in the face of such shameful behaviour towards Khwezi, while Gasa remarked, addressing Zuma, "[y]ou have not only fed into the most backwards sections of South African law, but you have deployed your training as an armed fighter in that arena against an unarmed individual."

Third, feminist commentators were decisive on where to lay the blame for both Khwezi's ongoing victimisation and general factors that convince women and girls to abstain from reporting rape and other forms of assault. Govender insisted that women and girls are dissuaded from reporting rape because of the high possibility that their revelations will be met with disbelief, the guaranteed occurrence of secondary rape in court and elsewhere as well as the resolution by a range of misogyny's footsoldiers to ensure their silence. Gail Smith noted that "rapists and abusers are enabled and protected by a society still intent on viewing women as unreliable, as liars and asking for rape," while her piece on the merits of the *amicus curiae* application insisted that Khwezi's "meltdown should be laid squarely at the door of those who allowed her previous sexual history to be admitted into evidence and those whose intransigence has seen the stalling of Sexual Offences Bill for eight years."

Fourth, feminist commentators noted the historic importance of this moment, not in the history of the ANC or Zuma or the presidential contest, in the ways that many mainstream media outlets decreed, but rather, for feminists, this was an important moment for women, for freedom and for reflection on forms of action. Khwezi's action has spurred this on at great cost, and this was to be supported, applauded and embraced. There may have been large masses of people outside the court terrorising Khwezi and the One in Nine Campaign in their purple shirts, but there was a host of women and men all over the country who, although not physically outside court, also metaphorically wore those same purple shirts.

This is a point that was driven home when the feminist poet and TV presenter, Lebogang Mashile donned a purple shirt at the end of the *L'attitude* eposide in which she tried to understand the vastly different motivations that shaped the actions of the women on both sides of the Khwezi/Zuma support lines.

Ludwig's reminder that "[j]ustice is not blind, neither are those who administer it", is a crucial one when dealing with rape and other manifestations of gender-based violence.

Many who couched our responses in feminist terms looked forward to a way out of the 'siege' women live under, as Wendy Isaack also calls it, because of gender-based violence. Pointing to the harassment that many feminist commentators received off-air and off-media, Ndashe argues that it is part of the attempts to make us docile, set back the women's movement and frighten us into 'remembering' our place as women. Nkutha argues that such treatment and disrespect for women's entitlement to privacy forces us further into ourselves by tiring us and making women think we can avert patriarchal attacks, forcing us as feminists to engage with anti-feminist possibilities.

Recognising the importance of the events at the trial and the surrounding theatre, various people chose to reject silence and to comment and intervene into the travesty that was the ongoing terrorising of Khwezi. They demonstrated that against all evidence, Khwezi had support and recognition, and that not all were represented by circulating, dominant constructions of 'ordinary people'.

These voices made indelible impressions on the national psyche and made it impossible for Zuma and his supporters to proceed as though he had wholescale support of people across the land. Indeed, those approaches critical of Zuma made it difficult to assess the precise levels of support for Zuma and blind regard for Khwezi and other women's integrity. It revealed that while South Africa was what Gail Smith called "a society that does not sufficiently protect or respect its women and girls", there was a mass of women and men of unpredictable numbers who were bruised and enraged by the status quo and were determined to forge new tools in the ongoing battle to end all forms of violence against women – physical and epistemic.

At the same time, there was a softening of voice in the midst of anger, as commentator after commentator spoke of the need for "empathy", solidarity among those of us who won't be passive audience to Khwezi's torture in order to better assert "our power with love and courage", to borrow Govender's phrase.

Feminists were not united in their suggestions for a way forward. Naylor and I made similar suggestions, with Naylor's pause requiring something akin to a pregnant silence which would allow us to arm ourselves with whatever tools we would need; while I imagined a re-arming that would be at once adaptive and historicised. Govender had suggested even prior to this that what was needed was a form of regrouping that would clarify our exact goals with as much precision as those systems we seek to dismantle.

Feminist commentators who publicly sided with Khwezi analysed here were unanimous in the fact of shared blame: that society enabled the Zuma case and countless other rapes and cases to play themselves out in the brutal ways that they did. Pityana was most far reaching in that he defined complicity as encompassing all those who did not actively dissociate themselves from Zuma and others like him, whether this meant retaining him as Vice-Chancellor (University of Zululand), allowing him to retain his honorary degrees (Durban Institute of Technology and Mangosuthu Technikon), or those previously honoured by these institutions who did not surrender their honorary degrees in protest.

For Pityana, the inaction by these institutions, like the silence critiqued by other feminist commentators, was complicity and active support for both Zuma and the theatrics of the trial within the court room and beyond.

Feminist commentators reshaped the terms of debate, and it is the rage and disregard for personal safety with which they acted that ensured that the media's construction of Khwezi's charge of rape and the trial she had to endure were contested. For feminist commentators, as Gasa said repeatedly on television appearances, "Zuma may not have been guilty of rape legally as per the decision of the court, but he was guilty of something." Feminists pointed to a variety of what constituted this "something". Beyond that, we attempted to unsettle the patriarchal elision of the woman whose life was made a living hell within the public sphere and beyond.

CHAPTER 6

Forked tongue on child rape

Every now and then, our national newspapers or television announce news of a gruesome rape that involves an old woman, a baby or a very small child. The entire nation seems to go into shock. Many call in to radio stations to discuss again and again the devastating incomprehensibility of such barbarity. Nobody understands what this is about, caller after caller declares, so that we can almost touch the sadness carried in these voices because we are a society falling apart.

A few people repeat the question as if it will make sense after just the right number of reiterations.

"How can a grown man be aroused by a baby?"

A few more people will declare again what a sick society we are. Some suggest that we need to 'return' to a better sense of ethics, or humanity or morality. It is never clear to me how far back in history we lost a grip on this 'return' being called for, and therefore what exactly is meant by such calls. However, the pain and frustration is one I share. I am pleased that we live in a country that refuses to be desensitised to the constant onslaught of rape, that we continue to be outraged, even if I find collective responses – beyond the shock and horror – deeply inadequate.

In 2001, Baby Tshepang was one such case. One night in Louisvale in the Northern Cape, twenty-two-year-old Lya Booysen went looking for her abusive boyfriend, David Potse. When she could not immediately find him, she decided to check his other (or ex) girlfriend's house. She was tired of waiting in bed for him. When she found him, he was raping Baby Tshepang. She was so shocked she dropped her match and had to light another one to confirm to herself what she had just seen. Potse continued to rape the nine-month-old child even as she stared at him in disbelief. Too uncomfortable to keep watching, she went back to her house where she resumed waiting for him in bed.

Tshepang was so damaged that she needed emergency surgery. Potse's semen was found in the baby's nappy as well as on the blankets. Booysen remained in an intimate relationship with Potse, and admitted to being both his girlfriend and still in love with him when she testified against him during the court proceedings in Upington. Potse was also either boyfriend or ex-boyfriend to Baby Tshepang's mother, in a complicated story of overlapping relationships.

In "Potse denies rape of Tshepang", Frans Coetzee writes:

> Potse testified under cross-examination that he would like to know how his semen came to be in the baby's rectum, on her diaper (that she had been wearing that evening) and on blankets and towels on the bed. He could not, however, explain how his semen had come to be on the evidence. [...] Investigating officer Inspector Marina van der Merwe testified that after it had been ascertained at the forensic laboratory that Potse's DNA profile matched the semen that had been found on the evidence, another blood sample was taken from him to make 'doubly sure'. The result was positive, once again.

In a case of excellent evidence collection, Potse's denials were rendered ridiculous. Investigators collected evidence and retested semen and blood samples to confirm the details contained in

Booysen's testimony that had placed him at the scene, in a very rare instance of a rape with witness collaboration. The case is as heartbreaking as it is unusually consistent for a rape case. The correlation between the witness's testimony and DNA evidence is quite remarkable. This is quite rare on several levels: most rapes do not have witnesses, and evidence collection is seldom as swift and effective as it was in this case.

Potse's denial is ridiculous for other reasons as well. Because he raped a baby, he is unable, like others charged with rape to argue that the sex was consensual, therefore he does not have access to an explanation. He then feigns ignorance at how his semen was found on the baby, as though someone other than himself deposited it there. Here, Potse tries to suggest that he was framed, an argument that has been used, cast as 'conspiracy' in high-profile cases in South Africa before. However, Potse does not have the qualities required to successfully build such an argument. This is an argument that only makes sense for powerful, prominent men who have many suspected enemies and whose power is evident for all to see. The reason Potse's attempts at denying raping Baby Tshepang ring hollow has everything to do with who the raped and rapist are. In addition to a witness and DNA evidence, Potse also fits the profile of who rapists are, and his choice of who to rape also fits circulating ideas of who is rapable.

Another remarkable aspect of this case is the behaviour and identity of the witness who is not swayed in her testimony. Potse and Booysen continue their relationship even as she testifies against him, something which seems counterintuitive. Her resolve to narrate what she witnessed does not temper her feelings for him: she returns to the bed they share so he may return after he has finished raping a baby. They are also both able to continue their relationship even as they stand on different sides on the law. Her decision to testify against him suggests her conviction that he should be held responsible for his illegal and harmful actions, and she decided not to protect him.

Yet all of this does not temper her decision to be with him in an intimate relationship, and presumably does not make her wonder about the safety of her own children around him. The reasons why he stays with her are equally puzzling. Even in a context where rape is counterintuitive, this case offers layers of challenges to our understanding of human behaviour, intimate partnerships and motivation.

Baby Tshepang's teenage mother, herself a rape survivor, had left her child with a relative who became drunk abandoning her child. We are told that the mother had also gone to drink before leaving Baby Tshepang with the negligent relative. After arrest, Potse is reported to have threatened further harm to mother and baby.

Potse's access to at least two girlfriends, as well as his choice of who to rape make it hard to hold onto ideas of rape as sex. Even those who believe that rape survivors invite rape would be hard pressed to show how a baby is capable of seduction and consent, hence the heightened sense of collective shock when we are confronted with news of children raped. Furthermore, Potse's decision to rape his girlfriend's child seems to confirm circulating ideas of child rapists as particularly depraved individuals.

Baby Tshepang's case received enormous attention with regular updates in the media as the baby underwent emergency treatment and extensive reconstructive surgery. Yet the sympathy reserved for the baby, and revulsion directed at Potse did not always temper the way in which Baby Tshepang's mother was shamed. The fact that she went drinking, leaving her child alone seemed to add fuel to the fire. Yet, anybody who takes care of little children knows that it is hard work and that any human being needs reprieve from such work. Middle-class women's magazines wax lyrical about the importance of finding 'me-time' away from children and work. This me-time is considered not a luxury, but a crucial respite and recovery time from hard work. It is time that allows women to continue to take on the multiple roles and responsibilities expected from them in our contemporary world. Yet, working-class and poor women have a less straightforward relationship with me-time in the public imagination. It matters little, it seems, that Baby Tshepang's mother did not leave her child unattended, even in a society that continues to hold onto the myth that most Black women have access to extended families who responsibly, and rightly, share parenting and childcare. She left her baby with another adult, and it is this second adult that then left the child alone. However, even though the behaviour of the second adult is clearly irresponsible since there are many dangers that could befall a child left unattended, she still cannot be held responsible for Potse deciding to rape the baby.

It is not only her community that blamed Baby Tshepang's mother for the rape of her baby, however. When her baby was taken away from her, and she followed in order to be close to Baby Tshepang who was no longer in her care, her new school mates repeatedly taunted and shamed her for her child's rape.

This case is one of compounded tragedies. The mother is herself a subject of intersecting forms of violence: poverty, her own rape and the trauma that stems from this, and the rape of her own baby for which she is then punished though the removal of the baby, placed with foster parents in Cape Town. Having initially followed her baby to Cape Town so she could retain some contact, Tshepang's mother later returned to Louisvale where she continues to live with all the reminders of perhaps her own rape, as well as the rape of her child.

In a story such as this, many people rush to outline the links between the socially degraded conditions of Baby Tshepang's life, the poverty, unemployment, helplessness of many young people with limited possibilities of self-improvement and escape, and some scholarship seems to confirm the likelihood of rape and other violent crime in conditions of constant degradation.

For her doctoral research, Amelia Ann Klein interviewed ten men convicted of raping children under the age of three. All Klein's interviewees were serving lengthy jail terms at the time of interview, and they ranged in age from 19 to 61. Klein is concerned with understanding the mentality of men such as these, and she chooses men who all fall into the publicly circulated profile of child rapist: unemployed at the time of raping the children, all school dropouts, three 'coloured' and seven 'black'. All her interviewees had suffered extreme institutional and personal violence as children. They all revealed stories of being beaten and verbally abused as children. Furthermore, each of these convicted child rapists had a 'heightened sexualised childhood'. In other words, Klein's research seemed to confirm that there is a cycle of abuse and sexual violence in child rapists' lives. The men studied in Klein's dissertation seem very similar in location to Potse, although we do not know enough about his childhood to confirm the presence of individual abuse or premature exposure to sexual content. He is similar to these men in racial classification, class position and impoverished background.

Klein's study also reveals that all the child rapists she interviewed also confess to feeling immense anger on the days of the rape, and that this anger was directed at men and women sometimes related to the children they raped. Some of the children were related to these men and women.

Klein was concerned with understanding the underlying factors for child rape, and perhaps contributing to the larger discussions about the kinds of interventions necessary. Although ten interviewees drawn from very similar personal backgrounds are a very small sample, Klein contributes to a larger scholarly literature on understanding violent offenders. This is not really my concern here, so those who share Klein's curiosity and particular interest would be well served reading the full dissertation and some of the literature she references that is interested in linked behavioural, psychological and psychiatric questions.

In her 2014 address to the Northern Cape Provincial Legislature at the beginning of the 16 days of no violence against women and children, the Public Protector, Advocate Thuli Madonsela reportedly noted the importance of ending the impunity with which violence against women happens, and understanding what turns people into monsters. For her, these two are linked. Impunity is a socially enabled phenomenon that comes from the absence of consequences for violence. Adv. Madonsela continued:

> [w]e assume people will stop killing women and children when we arrest them and send them to jail. Do you think someone who rapes a six month old baby is thinking about going to jail? [...] I will

never blame a woman for a man who rapes a child, for a man who beats up a woman. There is no reason anyone should beat up or rape a child. Children used to run around in Soweto and anywhere in society naked and nobody raped them. However, we must reduce opportunities for violence against women and children.

Madonsela argues for a multi-pronged approach: one that firstly, creates clear consequences for sexual and other gendered violence; secondly, eliminates excuses/justifications; and thirdly, deepens understandings of the kinds of deterrents that could work. For, if as she argues the threats of imprisonment – and its unlikelihood – are not the right deterrents, we need a clearer sense of what the appropriate deterrents are. Furthermore, Madonsela argues that solutions on how to minimise gender and sexual violence need further investigation, and these cannot invest in victim-blaming.

The Baby Tshepang case received enormous publicity and inspired a play and other work. Three recent cases received considerably less attention, and it is to these that I now turn. The point is not that they should have received as much attention as the Baby Tshepang case, but that they illuminate other dimensions of child rape in contemporary South Africa that help us build a bigger picture and perhaps move closer to the kind of understanding that Adv. Madonsela wishes for above.

The first is the case of the highly racialised case of rape at Jan Kempdorp High School, a Northern Cape boarding school, in February 2015, where several boys of different races watched as one of their own – a Black boy – was tied to a steel bed, and raped with a broomstick by six white pupils aged between 14 and 19 from the same school. Most reports noted that the rapists were all white Afrikaner boys, and that none of the boys who witnessed this violence intervened. The attackers shaved his head and painted him with a white substance, hung a board around his neck with his name and the name of his 'baas', while other boys watched, joked, laughed and recorded the event, during which the raped boy screamed and cried.

This was one of a series of disturbing incidents at South African schools at the beginning of 2015, and consequently, initial responses saw it as primarily a racist incident, alongside others reported at a Curro school that divided students into classes that has either Black or white students. However, revelations of the nature of the attack soon highlighted that it was a case of both race and sexual violence. It is a frightening case not just of brutal attack, but one that also seems to throw up other questions about direct complicity, violent masculinities and rape culture in this school.

While this student was tortured by four or six students, depending on which newspaper report one relies on, many more students watched his humiliation. At least one of them recorded the event and leaked it to the outside. Many times since this incident, we have had to ask questions about what is going on at the school, and to what extent versions of this kind of violence are possible at other schools. The Jan Kempdorp incident illustrates that much is wrong with the culture of masculinity, and the pressure to be violent among young people. It also shows the extent of racialised, gendered masculine culture in parts of our society. In a country where violent masculinities cross boundaries of race, but where some forms of violent expression are more likely to be performed by some men rather than others, it is clear that boys and young men are not safe.

This incident also shows the extent to which partaking in violent behaviour, as well as spectatorship and demonstrated support of brutality forms part of masculine peer pressure. At the same time, this violence is very deeply racialised, using the racist language of '*baas*' and well as other racist slurs reported in the media.

It does not seem that the students in question were particularly shocked by the events, nor did the obvious pain experienced by the boy who was raped move them to empathy. Silence about brutality is a requirement, and indeed, various journalists report hearing laughter and jokes as the scene unfolded.

While we may want to ask questions about how a majority of boys does not intervene as one child is raped by a few boys, it bears noting that this echoes general South African attitudes to violence in public spaces. The raped Grade 12 boy was a newcomer and it seems that it was generally accepted that he was to be initiated. This marked him as outsider, as initiation often does. Many school initiation rituals rest on the humiliation of the newcomer before he can be accepted as a member of the new school community. Initiation also demands secrecy by insiders on what happens, and patriarchal masculinity also values this ability to keep the business of men away from all others. It may well be that what was done to the new student did not differ radically from what other boys had been initiated to earlier. This is one way of explaining the failure of others to intervene, even if not to temper the extent of violence. Part of why this was so disturbing is because many adults like to pretend that initiation is harmless, that children cannot inflict long-lasting damage on one another. But secrecy, the ability to inflict violence and the ability to remain stoic in the face of violence are ideals that a society such as ours habitually celebrates. It is the stuff that 'real men' are made of, the fabric of heroism. This is partly why the young man's cries were met with laughter. All these boys would be familiar with the oft-cited reminder that real men do not cry when faced with pain. To cry then rendered him feminine in the same way that his public rape did.

The initiation worked racially in similar ways to its gendered meanings: on both planes, the Grade 12 student was being broken and rendered submissive. I am only separating the two to illustrate how the violence was as much about race as it was about gender, and that therefore quibbling about whether this was a race or gender crime misses the point. The point of school and associated initiations is to humiliate the newcomer, to bully him, and to then justify this inhumane behaviour in the name of fun. It is violence rendered enjoyable. In other words, during school initiations otherwise unacceptable behaviour is stripped of its consequences, and in a collective contract, those allowed to witness it pretend that humiliation is harmless teasing. South African Police Services spokesperson Dimakatso Mooi told Sbonokuhle Magcaba that "[i]t is alleged that they entered the room of the new pupil at around 9pm on Sunday as part of an initiation, but they went too far". In other words, even the police believe it is possible to humiliate within acceptable limits. The problem with this case is its excess, not the fact that violence and degradation are inherently harmful.

This is a fascinating double standard in a culture where we are starting to speak more against the bullying of children at school, and where increasing numbers of schools are teaching children to speak up against bullying and to report it so that it can be stopped. This rape lays bare the enactment of power to degrade, humiliate and break another. This is the work that rape always does. This is the function of violation.

Questions remain even after we have understood that the raced, gendered brutality enacted by these boys is not completely out of step with the place of violence elsewhere in South African society. Race and rape intertwine here in obvious ways, even though they intertwine often in less explicit ways. What is the status of a boy shamed by being raped in a deeply heterosexually violent society that speaks of all penetration as feminisation, where the most shameful position a man can assume is to be rendered like a woman? This desire to dominate, to render submissive, to render feminine and vulnerable, has echoes of the kind of colonial patriarchal theatre I traced in Chapter 2.

What do we make of public responses that posited that this was predominantly about race, those that argued it was really about gender and the resistance to see it as about both? The mother took her child out of the school in the end, charges were laid against the offending students who were then removed from this school and placed in another one. While the rape survivor has been provided with extensive access to therapy, questions remain about what the school could do to ensure that the context that enabled this rape is undone.

What can this school do with this instance as a lesson in changing the culture of the school?

What can other schools do to render what happened at Jan Kempdorp High School an impossibility at other schools?

The next case does not involve a school; it is that of a sixty-year-old-farmer from Stutterheim, William Martin Tindle Knoetze, who groomed and raped three children, now aged 9, 11 and 14, over several years. He and his thirty-five-year-old accomplice, who is also the mother of the nine-year-old, were convicted of 28 charges of sexually exploiting children and trafficking. Both were denied bail since they were taken into custody after arrest by the Hawks Organised Crime division on 12 January 2014.

Extensively covered in the Eastern Cape newspapers, *Daily Dispatch* and *The Herald*, but virtually absent from national media, this case and conviction presented more challenges to what goes on in child rape. The nine-year-old was the first girl Knoetze groomed and repeatedly raped, with her thirty-five-year-old mother's consent. Over time, Knoetze gradually manipulated the original girl to bring him two other girls for him to rape. He raped all three over several years, often forcing them to watch as he raped one, and sometimes forcing them to record these rapes.

The mother, who was Knoetze's co-accused in the court case, argued that Knoetze had promised to pay for the daughter's education in exchange for sexually violating the child. I am ambivalent about naming the mother and Knoetze's accomplice. On the one hand, as a convicted conspirator and accomplice to the three crimes of rape, sexual trafficking and child prostitution, she should be named. On the other hand, naming her identifies her daughter, and in the interest of protecting the privacy of her daughter, the rape survivor, her name should be withheld. This quandary about naming the nine-year-old's mother's seems to have plagued the journalists reporting on the case too, leading the same writers alternating revealing and/or withholding it in the news items reporting on the court case.

According to the SAPS Journal:

[t]he 9-year-old girl was drawn into this ordeal by her 35-year-old mother who gave her to Knoetze for sexual exploitation in return for cash. The girl was told to recruit to [*sic*] more girls, which she did. [...] The ordeal went on for a few years before one of the parents was curious about Knoetze's vehicle always picking her daughter up without her knowledge. When the mother interrogated the child, she burst into tears before she could open up about the shocking

details of her traumatic experience. [...] Knoetze apparently sexually exploited the children in return for R30.00. On some occasions, one of the girls would video Knoetze sexually exploiting her friend. The case has been postponed to 20 August 2014 in the Stutterheim Regional Court for a trial date. The suspects remain in custody.

The facts of the case are disturbing, and just as challenging for our ideas of how society works. In Baby Tshepang's case, her mother was shamed for failing to protect her child. In this case, the decision by the thirty-five-year-old mother to deliberately put her child in danger, repeatedly, and to further endanger more children defies all understanding in our society of what parental love and responsibility entail.

In May 2015 they both pleaded guilty to child prostitution, trafficking and sexual exploitation.

The public responses, like the quoted commentary by police and court officers highlighted the palpable shock at a mother who would willingly surrender her child to be raped. The mother's logic of thinking that payment for her education justified her child's rape did nothing to soften the incomprehension. In patriarchal societies motherhood and mothering are mythologised around inherent empathy, nurturing and selflessness, especially when it comes to a woman's own children. Here was a mother who defied both expectation and logic: a monster mother. However, even if we resist mythical motherhood, reflecting on this child's absolute vulnerability is devastating.

How do we understand this story, given our expectations that children are raped in secret, away from the protective eyes of the parents tasked with loving and protecting them? If we cannot assume that children are safer with present parents against rapists, how should we think about what it means to protect children whose own parents make them accessible to predators?

The story highlights different parenting choices. It came out and was investigated, prosecuted and resolved because another mother grew suspicious of Knoetze's interest in her daughter. This mother, unlike the first, failed to understand why this man kept picking her child up when she was not around, questioned the old white man's interest in the company of children, and did not take Knoetze's apparent friendliness at face value. Because she would not stop asking her daughter, the child eventually cried and told her mother what was happening. I am sure she had hoped that her suspicions were mere paranoia. Unlike the first mother, this one was determined that Knoetze be held responsible for the harm inflicted on these children.

Magistrate Ignatius Kitching sentenced Knoetze:

> to 15 years for each rape count, 12 years for the human trafficking charges and 10 years for the sexual exploitation charges. The sentences are to run concurrently. [...] Kitching then ordered that Knoetze's name be added to the Sexual Offenders Register. [...] As he walked to the holding cells, a teary Knoetze looked to the packed gallery and said *ndicel' uxolo* (I am sorry).

His accomplice, and mother of the youngest of Knoetze's victims, "was sentenced to 12 years for human trafficking charges and 10 years for the sexual exploitation charges. Her sentences are to run concurrently."

I am not sure what kind of sentencing would fit the kind of damage done to these children by Knoetze and his accomplice, and I am aware that sentencing cannot be determined by public sentiment. Nonetheless, sentences served concurrently, along with the six-year sentence handed to another serial rapist, former tennis star Bob Hewitt, a case to which I now briefly turn, seem to fly in the face of the crisis.

Bob Hewitt, the famous former tennis champion was also recently convicted of raping several children he coached at tennis over many years. Erin Bates writes that Hewitt's paedophilia was 'an open secret' in the tennis fraternity, and reveals that:

> sources close to the case say many more possible victims of Hewitt's abuse – who live in South Africa, the United States, and

New Zealand – have not come forward with details on alleged assaults that occurred when he was their adult tennis coach and they were minors.

Seventy-five-year-old Hewitt was sentenced to six years in prison and the payment of R100 000 to fund campaigns against violence against women and children. This sentence was for the rape of his two students, Suellen Sheehan and Theresa Tolken, now adults, and the indecent assault of a complainant who may not be named. Judge Bert Bam noted that he was convinced that the state has built a strong case, continuing to point out that:

> in cases of the rape of a minor, an accused would normally face a life sentence. However, because the crimes occurred in the 1980s and 1990s, legislation at the time did not have a minimum sentence. He said that the punishment has to fit both the criminal and the crime, and that mercy is always an element the court should consider.

The judge seems to be saying that he was unable to sentence Hewitt to a much higher sentence because of the complications posed by the period during which the crimes were committed by Hewitt. The last sentence in the excerpt above suggests that the judge wanted to both show the importance of being punitive and having mercy on Hewitt.

The judge noted that Hewitt had shown no remorse from the 1980s by assaulting another student in the 1990s, that although he was not concerned with Hewitt re-offending because of his age, retribution was necessary, noting first, that "sending a man soon to be an octogenarian to a prison sentence would be an incredibly severe punishment, but that it was not uncommon in South African law," and second, that a younger Hewitt would have received "more than 20 years behind bars." Whereas Hewitt had attempted to use his age as a mitigating factor in sentencing, the judge dismissed this, by declaring "[n]o rapist or violator of children should be able to hide behind his age."

The judge seems to be saying both that Hewitt could be sentenced to more years – although not a life sentence – if he were younger *and* that age should not be an excuse that allows Hewitt to escape imprisonment.

Sports bodies responded swiftly to Hewitt's court case. In November 2012, Mark Stenning, executive director of the International Tennis Hall of Fame in Boston was quoted as saying that a unanimous decision to suspend Hewitt was reached by the 25-member executive committee.

The Australian-born grand-slam champion, who moved to South Africa after marrying a South African, was a powerful man that many parents paid to coach their children in an attempt to give them the best possible opportunities. Instead, he used his power to groom, assault and rape some of these girls. Although some of the children he abused spoke to global media outlets, only three came forward for the South African trial.

It is worth noting that the cases discussed in this chapter are not the norm in cases of child rape, where evidence is collected and testimony found that is deemed reliable and sufficient to secure a conviction. Dumisile Nala, executive officer at Childline South Africa insists that rapists and other sex offenders often walk free because:

[i]f a prosecutor feels that the child is not ready to testify, we encourage them to refer them to us. We would then spend time in therapy with the kids. This has to be done with great sensitivity. Eventually when we build trust, we explain to them why they have to go to court, who they will see there and what would be expected from them. [...] When accused sex offenders are released they often return to the communities where they committed their crimes and tell communities that they have been vindicated by the court. [...] The children have to live with the trauma of having their abusers close by, again. But, they too want to move on with their lives so we rarely see the charges against the reoffenders reinstated after the children reach an age where they can testify more comfortably.

Children who speak of their rape are in a very precarious position therefore, according to Nala, since they may live to see their rapist walk free. Many prosecutors do not request assistance from those qualified to work with children. Consequently, many children's rapes are thrown out of court since young children may make unreliable witnesses and in the absence of DNA evidence, prosecutors decide that a case cannot be made. The Siqalo settlement community in Mitchells Plain about which Daneel Knoetze writes "Child rape case – how poor families struggle for justice" had discovered that Madala, a man in his seventies, admired by the community because he loved children, and considered the communal grandfather had been raping at least three little girls between 5 and 7 years old. The community had responded with rage on the discovery, dismantling and burning Madala's shack and belongings and banishing him from the community. When faced with the prosecutor's and the NPA's frustration at the answers given by the small children, and therefore the prospect of seeing Madala escape prosecution and being set free, these community members approached Childline South Africa, who were able to assist.

Through examining various cases of child rape that successfully came to court, several things have emerged. First, is that children are not raped by monsters. They are often raped by those entrusted with their safety: nice men who seem grandfatherly, a mother's boyfriend, school mates, a celebrated sportsman, and their mother's employer who has children of the same age. Child rapists are not monsters, nor are they all necessarily young men from impoverished backgrounds. It is difficult to create a reliable profile of a child rapist, as the diversity in this chapter shows. There is more diversity in the real world than I have been able to capture here. The rapist is also often a family member, not just someone merely considered a family member.

Although children are set up in the credibility/plausibility connection in Chapter 1 as the most believable rape survivors, this does not always translate into harsh sentencing. Children may be unable to testify for themselves in ways that ensure a conviction and consequently their cases may stall. Contrary to public gender talk, there is no significant difference between those who rape adults and those who rape children: it may be young adults or old men, poor men or wealthy powerful men, peers or those who are idealised in their communities. Those who rape babies and children, like those who rape adult women and men, can be anybody. They are usually known and trusted by the children they raped, and a significant amount of grooming is used for children.

At the same time, although child and baby rapes are often presented as the most horrendous forms of rape – a comparison that is in itself problematic – sentencing is not necessarily harsher for those convicted of rape, as the cases analysed in this chapter show. Indeed, in August 2011 a submission by Nicole Fritz for the Southern Africa Litigation Centre showed that Justice Mogoeng, then nominated to the top post in the Constitutional Court, which he holds currently, had a record of minimising child rape, with Fritz quoting from *S v Sebaeng (CA 16/2007) [2007] ZANWHC 25* (22 June 2007) where Justice Mogoeng had noted that the fourteen-year-old survivor had not acted as though she was in pain when she arrived at her grandmother's house after the rape, and furthermore that:

> [o]ne can safely assume that [the accused] must have been mindful of her tender age and thus so careful as not to injure her private parts, except accidentally, when he penetrated her. That would explain why the child was neither sad nor crying when she returned from the shop notwithstanding the rape. In addition to the tender approach that would explain the absence of serious injuries and the absence of serious bleeding, he bought her silence and cooperation with Simba chips and the R30.00.

In another case, this time *S v Serekwane (175/05) [2005] ZANWHC 52* (1 August 2005), Justice Mogoeng had concurred with the reduction of a five-year sentence to a three-year sentence for the rape of a seven-year-old, noting that the "injury" the child rape survivor raped by her father's friend "sustained is not serious", continuing, "she sustained a bruise on her vestibule. Although there was no direct evidence led, she must have suffered some psychological trauma, as a result of this incident."

These are two examples from the submission which showed a record of leniency in cases of rape and violence against women, including femicide. As Anna Majavu argued in "How a rape judgement fails vulnerable children all over South Africa", there are many other similar cases of child-rape sentences reduced because the rape itself was not serious.

CHAPTER 7

Rape myths

In our obsessive talk about rape and other forms of gender-based violence, several myths about rape get high circulation. We hear them in private conversations as well as in public ones. Sometimes they pass unchallenged, while at other times they are passionately defended.

Rethinking and debunking rape myths is an important part of the conversation of how to bring down the rape statistics and how to create a world without rape. Addressing them allows us to move closer to a world in which rape is taken seriously, where survivors can be supported and recover and where rape is dissuaded rather than excused.

It is also important to note that rape myths do dangerous work. They can embolden perpetrators and re-traumatise victims and survivors. Rape myths and excuses are at the heart of what is keeping rape culture intact. If we accept that it is time to render all forms of gendered violence genuinely illegitimate in all spaces we occupy, then it follows that to do so we need to stop making excuses, that we take up the challenge to constantly debunk rape myths wherever we encounter them because all gender-based violence is brutality, a form of gender war against survivors' bodies and psyches.

The myths and excuses are listed in no particular order. I simply address them in the order in which they came to me in the book's shortest chapter.

Perpetrators are monsters who are abusive all the time.
This is an expectation that many people have, and consequently one of the most enduring rape myths. It rears its head often when a survivor's narrative is being questioned. Rapists and other abusers are normal people. They can be very loving and gentle to those close to them. Remember the serial rapists who were upset by the prospect of their loved ones being treated the way they treat women? That is not so unusual. There is no consensus on what characteristics are to be found in someone who is likely to rape or be abusive in any other way. The only thing that rapists have in common is the refusal to accept no.

Rape is inappropriate sex.
Rape is not sex. It is:

> an act of non-consensual sexual violence, directed against a woman or someone constructed as feminine. It is an expression of masculine power and female vulnerability. Vulnerability, indeed, seems to be the theme which occurs in all the studies I have read of raped women, as Yvette Abrahams clarifies.

Rape is not about sex. It is about power. It is a highly painful experience, a highly "traumatic experience and like other serious traumas, it has negative effects on those who survive it. Rape is usually experienced as life-threatening and as an extreme violation of the self," as Desiree Hansson reminds us. One of the methods in which feminists have sought to shift the ways in which people and the legal system treat rape is through the recognition of Rape Trauma Syndrome (RTS).

The symptoms of RTS are wide-ranging and can find expression through the body, behavioural change and emotionally. Some survivors feel excessively cold, experience gynaecological problems, sore throats, tension headaches, abdominal and back pain, insomnia or excessive drowsiness, loss and increase in appetite, dramatic changes in their menstrual cycles, increased pains, nausea, discharges, sexually transmitted infections, cuts, bladder infections and other injuries on the body depending on the events of the rape. Rape survivors may change their behaviour by isolating themselves or going out more than before, may have difficulty concentrating, agitation, anxiety, depression, loss of interest in things that were important to them before the rape, oversensitivity to things that did not bother them before the rape, and may become easily startled or frightened. Rape survivors can also experience sexual disruption or significant shifts in sexual behaviour. I have known women who lost all interest in sex after the rape as well as women who reported that they wanted to have sex with their partners as part of trying to return to normal and to establish that their partners still found them sexually attractive. At the same time, I have witnessed previously solid relationships disintegrate completely in the aftermath of rape. Some survivors experience flashbacks, develop phobias or turn to substances that allow them to escape. Others develop 'traumaphobias', phobias both temporary and longer term that are triggered by rape trauma which may not have existed prior to being raped.

Although different combinations of these are experienced, feelings of shame, guilt and self-blame are very common. Those who seem to continue as though unaffected are in denial, in a state of shock or trying to block out the rape. Surviving means learning to confront at your own pace, and to live with the rape having happened. Counselling also helps the survivor move through the various stages of trauma to healing.

There is a proper way to respond to being raped.
This myth brings to mind a cartoon by Voices Rising that used to appear in many feminist publications until about a decade ago. It is a myth that places undue burdens on rape survivors, and this is what the cartoon captures so well. It has a policeman and a man dressed in legal garb with wig, bow blouse and black robe standing alongside each other facing forward with speech bubbles

above their heads. The police officer's speech bubble says "If you want to survive a rape, don't fight back". The lawyer's bubble says "If you don't fight back, you must have wanted it."

There is no one way to respond to rape, nor is the criminal justice system consistent in what it expects from survivors and those who seek to support them. Instead, globally when it comes to rape, survivors often confront mixed messages.

Navi Pillay notes that the legal justice system still treats women who report rape and other forms of violation in ways that are shaped by the myths that suggest that women's 'sexual proclivities' are responsible for their violation, that women are perpetually sex objects and men are both disarmed and helpless against their natural desires for women's bodies, that women who have had sex before somehow cause the rape and also "that victims resist and suffer physical injury to prove that they had not consented. This ignores what psychologists and women tell us, that a non-consenting woman may well freeze, or co-operate out of fear of injury."

Rape is when a man rapes a woman using his penis to forcibly penetrate her vagina.
Rape is a violation that can be inflicted on anyone. And the use of non-biological weapons is not unheard of. As Rape Crisis Cape Town notes:

> [i]t is important to realise that rape can happen between same-sex partners and that thinking that rape can only happen between a man and a woman is also a myth. In certain instances women have been known to rape men but at Rape Crisis we have found this to be the exception rather than the rule and so we base our comments on rape between a man and a woman realising that each rape is unique even as we generalise about it.

Rape myths are just harmless ignorance.
They actually have real effects. Sometimes they have implications for who is held accountable/responsible. They create the image and an idea of 'real' rape and notion of mostly false rape as

abundant. This is inaccurate since rapes differ and false reports are generally the exception. Rape myths enable rape culture to thrive, sometimes enable the secondary victimisation of survivors and create the female fear factory. Some rape myths shame the survivor instead of offering support towards healing.

Real rape victims/survivors lay charges with the police because they have nothing to lose.

Often when a woman breaks her silence on rape, or when several women accuse the same man of sexual assault, various people who are not directly involved insist that those 'real rape victims' seek out police help since they have nothing to hide.

This is possibly one of the most dangerous rape myths anywhere. Research findings on rape reporting show that only a small percentage of those who are sexually violated report the crime to the police for a range of reasons from stigma, to fear of secondary victimisation, to knowledge of how low the chances of a successful prosecution are.

A 2005 Medical Research Council report showed that only one in nine women reported their rape to the police, whereas South African Police Service 2010/2011 reported that of the 66 000 cases of sexual assault reported to them between April 2010 and March 2011, half were perpetrated against children.

In "The War at Home", a 2011 joint research report by the Medical Research Report and Gender Links stated that roughly one in every twenty-five rapes are reported to the police in Gauteng. The authors predicted that there were fluctuations in this number in other provinces, with even lower rates of reporting in some provinces based on previous research findings.

Many forms of rape and sexual assault are normalised, or, to quote from One in Nine Campaign's publication 2012 "*We were never meant to survive: violence in the lives of HIV+ women*":

[s]ome forms of sexual violence, too, are socially constructed as acceptable because of the nature of the relationship within which they occur. Thus, a distinction is often made between 'rape' and

coercion to have sex, with the latter comprising the vast majority of sexual violence – those not involving 'overt' violence and where the perpetrators are members of the family or boyfriends and husbands.

There are various reasons why rape reporting is lower than the incidents of rape. Rape Crisis counts among these reasons various consequences that may result from being identified as a survivor, including but not limited to loss of financial support if the rapist is a family member, stigma, protecting loved ones from the consequences of the rapist being arrested, lack of access to required services whether police stations are far or some other impediment, fear of further violence by the rapist and those associated with him, not being believed, and the knowledge that the legal justice system has very few successful cases of prosecution, with Rape Crisis reporting 4% conviction rates in Gauteng and 7% in the Western Cape:

> In 2010/2011 Rape Crisis saw over 2 700 rape cases for direct support and the number increased to over 5 000 in 2011/2012. Some of these survivors had reported the matter and some had not. Those who had reported, experienced the justice system in many instances as helpful, with distinct pockets of excellence where dedicated officials went the extra mile on their behalf and made them believe that their case was being taken very seriously. But even when this was the case in one area of the CJS [Criminal Justice System], the opposite was usually true in another, with the result that there was no one case where all parts of the system – police services, health facilities and courts – worked well and in a coordinated fashion to ensure a successful conviction.

Rape is about male arousal and the need to have sex.
Rape is sometimes enacted with objects other than the penis, yet:

> [v]iolence against women is seen as an individual male aberration rather than a social problem. The social reality for women is that they face the potential threat of violence and rape in their lives.

The life of men is comparatively secure – they can walk in parks or commune at night without this fear," as Navi Pillay reminds us.

Dressing a certain way or being visibly drunk invites rape.
Women are raped in all manner of dress and undress, and often by people they know. There is no correlation between how a woman dresses and her ability to escape rape. Rape is about power not seduction, and men are not helpless children but adults with the power to self-control. Women should be free to dress as they please without being blamed for what might be done to them.

Rapists are strangers who abduct women in public and rape them in unknown places.
This one is not quite a myth. While globally most survivors know their rapists, there are also cultures of women being abducted from public places and being raped, either by a single man or gang raped. There are also established histories of women attacked under conditions of war. Various chapters in this book revisit this notion that women are not likely to be raped by a stranger to show that in South Africa many rapes have fallen into just this category from slave rape to colonial rape to jackrolling.

Sex workers cannot be raped.
Anybody can be raped. Just because people work in an industry where sex is for sale does not mean they are available for sex with all people all the time. Sex workers are capable of saying no, of not wanting to have sex, and therefore they *can* be raped. This is especially so since rape is not about sex but about power and vulnerability. Sex workers can be particularly vulnerable since they work in a criminalised sector and therefore cannot claim the same resources that other workers can.

There is also a wealth of research that shows that a significant percentage of sex workers become prostitutes through trafficking and rape. In other words, not only can they be raped, but sometimes their entry into this work is through sexual violence which may continue.

Women are accidentally raped because they play hard-to-get.
Playing hard-to-get is a patriarchal construct that enables rape culture. For as long as it is taken for granted that women are playing hard-to-get when they turn down men's heterosexual advances, they can be pursued in a courtship process/process of the heterosexual chase that ultimately changes the refusal into acquiescence. The phenomenon of being 'friend-zoned' is allied to this. It suggests that there is something humorously amiss when a woman chooses to be friends with a man who desires a sexual/romantic relationship with her. The 'friend-zone' is mythologised in global popular culture as a form of punishment from which heterosexual men are constantly trying to escape in order to successfully attain romantic-partner status. Yet, if women are adults, indeed human beings of any age, then they are capable of saying yes when they so desire. Even if a woman is 'playing hard-to-get', violating her cannot be an accident.

Rape looks a certain way. It leaves a specific imprint on the body.
Jane Bennett continues to ask:

> what kind of 'physical,' referential pain is inflicted by rape? A body is as visibly 'whole' after rape as before. There are likely to be abrasions, bruises – perhaps worse if a 'weapon' was used – but these markings are mere witnesses to the presence; they only hint at the 'wound' itself in a script that lends itself as easily to the description of an unfortunate accident as to the (sometimes) temporary annihilation of the semiotic process through which a woman may make sense of herself.

There are others.

It is time to stop these acts of war against women's psyches and bodies. It is time to stop giving airplay to the excuses that make rape and all other forms of gender-based violence seem harmless, excuses that allow it to stay normal. Excuses keep gender-based violence: violence against women, girls, boys, gender non-conforming people, queers of all hues in place. They hold the survivors hostage while letting the perpetrators off.

In other words, when we make excuses on rape, we provide

cover for brutal men to violate all others with impunity. Slut-shaming, rape-culture, intimate femicide, sexual harassment, sexual trafficking, the forced marriage of girls to men old enough to be their (grand)fathers, all rely on excuses to make them seem acceptable, and to make rape seem harmless.

Excuses say it is fine to punish a survivor for the short skirt she wears, fine to excuse the male professor who sexually harasses his students and colleagues, overly sexualising them, making inappropriate comments that the woman student is obliged to think of as compliments to stay alive. It is *not* fine.

Excuses say violence against Black women is part of generalised violence against Black people and that brutal men cannot be called the monsters they are when they rape, beat their partners and make excuses. This is another really dangerous excuse. *All* men, no matter what race, class or religion have patriarchal power and can choose to brutalise and get away with it.

Excuses say that only working-class Black men rape and that white women and gender non-conforming people do not have to deal with this from white middle- and upper-class educated men. Chapter 2 and 6 have many examples of white men who rape as individuals and as part of armies. I've also given many examples of men who are not poor who have been accused or convicted of rape.

Excuses make violence against women possible – they are part of the complicated network that says women are not human, so our pain is generalised, unimportant, so we give violent men permission to keep all those they deem vulnerable, such as women, men, and gender non-conforming people or children.

When we make excuses we become the perpetrators and their allies. It is important to redefine what justice means, recognising that it lies not in political speeches, the mention of non-sexism at the bottom of stationery, for many women it is not in the criminal justice system.

Survivors of gender-based violence are the world's majority; they walk the streets all day everywhere, sit next to you in class, they are the person you are busy falling in love with, they are your sister, your best friend, lover, mother, daughter, your teacher.

CHAPTER 8

Violent masculinities and war talk

There is a connection between rape culture, the manufacture of female fear and violent masculinities. It is as follows: violent masculinities create a public consciousness in which violence is not just acceptable and justified, but also natural and desirable. They glamorise violence in a variety of masking manoeuvres that seduce spectators into mythologising violence. In other words, while watching violence, we imagine we are watching something else: humour, freedom, play and healthy assertions of self.

In a country such as South Africa, where violence is so embedded in many processes of communication, and not just contestation, it is possible to misread violence as something else, to cease seeing some manifestations of it. We attain fluency in the grammar of violence and begin to either celebrate violent ways of being or cease to think of them as violent altogether. This is particularly true as our violence-saturated public and private worlds now rub up against global machinery that is gun-toting and celebrates hypermasculinity in film, wars and some musical genres. This glamourisation also makes violence appear as if it is the same thing as a radical transformative politics, thereby reinforcing a culture – an atmosphere – that is about making threats to others: sometimes other men, but also women. Sometimes these threats of violence are direct and at other times they are translated into regimes that police women and vulnerable others, telling women what body-styling choices are legitimate and which not, shaming people for their body-styling choices, sexual orientation and gender non-conformity.

This pervasive culture of violence also means that when others defend themselves, or stand up for themselves by questioning violent men, the latter groups become available for attack by the defenders of violent men. For example, when Oscar Pistorius was on trial for killing his girlfriend, Reeva Steenkamp, legions of the Paralympian's mostly women fans called themselves "Pistorians" and proceeded to tweet, facebook and elsewhere hashtag a variety of flattering comments on Pistorius, across social media. They also defended him against any criticism by trolling social media and attacking those who were critical of, or angered, by Pistorius's killing of Reeva. They were focused on stifling dissent and anger that Pistorius had just killed a woman, at how the court case was proceeding, the intersections of gender, class and race in aspects of the defence and the manner in which this killing intersected with the high statistics of femicide. For the Pistorians, if the Paralympian did not intend to kill Ms Steenkamp, then there was no cause for alarm. This defence of a man that even the Pistorians have to admit is a violent man, with his guns in public and private spaces, as well as all those bullets shot into his bathroom, is an example of how space is made for violent masculinities to take centre stage, and war talk is legitimised.

This was the same kind of manifestation that we saw outside court during the Jacob Zuma rape trial, but also one that went far beyond that to threaten some of Zuma's detractors to utter statements that have ranged from insisting they would defend Zuma with all their might (as though he is in physical danger) to insisting that they would kill for him. The creation of a public culture saturated with threats of violence also serves to silence dissent and strengthen the female fear factory.

The fact of the matter is that Zuma is the president of a democratic country, and he is therefore legitimately subjected to scrutiny, as are many other elected officials, such as the former leader of the opposition, Helen Zille, and the leader of the new smaller opposition party, Julius Malema. Yet, while in principle our public figures agree that they may be questioned, in practice some of them respond with threatening or violently dismissive language when questioned. Even more troublingly, many of those who come to their defence do so with such viciousness that, across the spectrum, has become the norm.

Before I attend to some examples of what I mean by violent masculinities and war talk, let me pay attention to what it is not. Hypermasculinity goes hand in hand with violent masculinities, misogyny and war talk. However, not all claims to masculinity are in and of themselves assertions of violence, or at least the specific kind of violence I am concerned with in this chapter. It is possible for individuals and groups of men to lay claim to adult masculine identity without being hypermasculine. Hypermasculinity is a heightened claim to patriarchal manhood, to aggression, strength and sexuality. It is effectively manhood on metaphoric steroids.

Therefore, even as I elect here to identify and problematise those who most consistently demonstrate war talk in South African public life, it is important to note that, historically, there are wide-ranging masculinities in South Africa, and historic claims to manhood that formed part of the political left. Raymond Suttner's scholarship reminds us of the further complicated ways in which assertions of African masculinity can be expressions of both freedom and patriarchal power. Under colonialism and apartheid, adult Africans were designated boys and girls, legally and economically infantilised. It is therefore important to be attentive to the layered meanings of asserted manhood.

Suttner reflects on this phenomenon thus:

[t]he infantilisation of Africans and men in particular links to or seeks to justify political domination by designating Africans as a race of children. [...] In reading African assertions of manhood, therefore, we need to understand it as a challenge not only to a childlike status but as symbolising wider rejection of overlordship. [...] The assertion of manhood is in this context a claim for freedom.

He also notes:

[n]otions of masculinity are essentially conditional, contested, ambiguous or contradictory and have varied over time and at any particular moment and within any particular experience.

In other words, there is a long history of claiming manhood as a state of being an adult – which is different from, although sometimes linked to, the patriarchal denunciation of 'emasculation'. In this history that Suttner writes of, claims to manhood were a rejection of the specific infantilisation of African men.

Thus, although much scholarship reads assertions of manhood as straightforward patriarchal statements, Suttner insists that context demands attention to the complicated work at play here, even when such assertions are patriarchal. In other words, it is not the mere claiming or evoking of manhood that matters, but also the specific ways in which contexts inflect the meanings of such assertions of specific masculinities. Understanding this is key to appreciating the varied, and specific, ways in which apartheid was always a gendered project. Consequently, anti-apartheid initiatives were also gendered in precise ways, not all patriarchal. But even the patriarchal ones were not always engaged in war talk and the celebration of violent masculinities.

It is exactly the complicated combination of struggle parlance and violent masculinities that leads to the unregulated effects of the spectacular masculinities that I discuss in this chapter. The sometimes muted, at other times ambivalent, responses to such hypermasculine performance are also influenced by the collective

155

memory that is indexed by the masculinities under discussion.

Suttner's warning about how to make sense of performed and/ or claimed ANC masculinities is important here. He notes that:

> [i]f full weight is not given to the denial of manhood, one cannot give meaning to a claim of manhood. [...] one cannot read off gender relations or a negative relationship to women from the assertion of manhood in itself [...] the assertion of manhood has no self-evident and timeless meaning. The struggle to be a man meant the struggle for dignity and reclaiming of rights and to be treated as an adult human being. This is something that needs to be read into any analysis of ANC masculinities.

In other words, different meanings can be attached to claimed manhood. Under apartheid, such declarations are assertions of adult agency, which is defiant in the face of an infantilising regime. It is thus difficult to read the mere statement of manhood as automatically indexing patriarchal relationships with women. As Suttner warns, superficial attention to history, and therefore context, leads to easy answers that do not hold up to scrutiny.

Suttner's warning notwithstanding, assertions of masculinity need not function on a single plane. It is possible to both profess gendered adulthood to the apartheid state and imply hierarchical relationships between genders, and this is not just true of ANC masculinities. When the claim to manhood was also accompanied by masculinist organisational culture, or when the manhood being claimed is a de facto patriarchal masculinity, then of course we can read patriarchal – and therefore a negative relation to women, in addition to a critique of white supremacist minoritisation of men. This is particularly clear in the oft-repeated claim by Black men in the left drawn from various liberation movements in Africa and its diaspora that they have been 'emasculated' and need to assert masculinity over women, and that women should rightfully enable this return to masculinity. While this emasculation discourse challenges the infantilisation that Black men suffer in racist white regimes, this claim to recover from emasculation very often requires the performance of hypermasculinity that women are expected to support as part of enabling these men to attain manhood. In some of its most brutal manifestation, it directly trivialises sexual violence by these men. In the essays collected in *Frank Talk 10*, Andile Mngxitama and Athi Joja argue that Black men cannot inflict violence on Black women, firstly, because the former attains the status of 'women' under white supremacy and can therefore not access, let alone exert, patriarchal power, and second, because Black life is so generally violent, when Black men rape Black women this cannot lead to the kinds of trauma that sexual violence produces. In other words, ironically, they, like colonial legislators argue that Black women are impossible to rape. They do so in a collection of writings that ostensibly offers a critique of white violence on Black bodies. Their war talk is most evident in the contempt demonstrated by these two writers towards Black feminist activism and writing, and most especially Black lesbian feminist work; Mngxitama and Joja do so while also rhetorically going to great lengths to position themselves within a radical Black tradition. I have dealt with patriarchal inversion before, in an earlier chapter of this book.

The widespread reading of left-wing masculinities as exclusively, or predominantly, assertions of political agency, codified as heroism, enables the spectacular masculinities I critique in this chapter. But the left does not have monopoly over hypermasculinity. Both the militaristic, gun-toting culture of Afrikaner masculinity that was revealed to be embodied in figures like Pistorius as well as the triple threat of laddism, raunch culture and 'retrosexism' of white English-speaking public masculinities stage hypermasculinities. Dominique Rizos's work explores this, especially in the article "Lad magazines, raunch culture and the pornification of South African media" and her longer research project "Lad magazines, raunch culture and the increasing pornification of South African media." She shows the manner in which ostensibly benign and ironic masculine positions on feminism (laddism) actually code misogynist cultures, in other words war talk; in such media not marked as pornographic, "the idea of female objectification and male dominance is esteemed." Although laddism and raunch culture do not immediately appear violent, they are in fact staging of hypermasculinity. In the midst of songs about machine guns and guns fired through locked doors, it is important to remember that hypermasculinity also claims patriarchal manhood through patriarchal sexual cultures. As Rizos shows, in the case of raunch culture, this violence is both pornographic and normalises pornography. When she writes of pornography, she refers specifically to the violent sexual representation and framing of sexuality, not to unhindered sexual expression. This is also the sense in which I spoke of empire as a pornographic project, in the same manner as Dabydeen in an earlier chapter.

Violent masculinities reveal themselves in contests between forms of masculinity. Here, self-authorising performance of patriarchal masculinity unfolds in public spaces, where such performance hints at masculine violence or a contest between forms of manhood. When Jacob Zuma sang the hugely popular struggle toyi-toyi song *"umshini wam"* when he was charged with rape, he understood the power of heroic masculinity, having previously embodied it himself, and knew how to reference it to shame Khwezi.

Many feminist commentators pointed this out in public forums, including the press, at the time. Zuma's behaviour and choice of toyi-toyi song were inappropriate because they located him in the realm of heroic and militant masculinity, and the complainant, by implication, was placed in opposition to struggle masculinity. His performances folded Zuma's spectacular masculinism into the realm of the heroic, an idiom recognisable to most South African audiences. While some commentators fixated on the symbolic phallic presence of a gun to stand in for a penis in this instance, it is important to note that even if he had sung a different struggle song, the performance of hypermasculinity would have been possible. This is because the struggle was a just fight against an oppressive regime. When a struggle song that has such resonance is sung in the context of a powerful man accused of rape, it takes on symbolic value to cast the complainant as an enemy. More importantly, it casts her as the enemy of all those who are able to sing the song.

In other words, Khwezi becomes the enemy and safe to treat in any way because she is an enemy that has been marked with associations that come from apartheid. All righteous, freedom-loving people are reminded of the wound of apartheid, incited to anger, always ready because the apartheid memory is too fresh in all of us, so that Khwezi becomes possible to burn. It is therefore not a huge leap from seeing her as a political enemy, like an askari might have been, to chanting "burn the bitch".

In his essay, "Jacob Zuma and the Family", which was first published in *Sunday Times* on 6 March 2003, Njabulo Ndebele declared that he was intrigued, pained and revolted by Zuma's self-representation. In calling for his machine gun as he faced his rape trial, Zuma showed how he had mastered the art of the spectacle. Among the immediate associations that this song would have evoked were the militancy associated with the armed struggle, the anger that was underlined as the appropriate response to apartheid, as well as the importance of taking up arms as self-defence against, and attack on, a brutal white supremacist regime. This song would have reminded even those only marginally involved in the struggle of the marches that brought South African cities to a halt during the transition to democracy. Being from both the recent and distant past, the song invited the public to view Zuma's prosecution as unjust. Indeed, it equated the complainant in the rape trial with an oppressive past.

When a man who is charged with rape sings a song like "*umshini wam*" convincingly, he asserts that the struggle is not over, another facet that resonated with many Black South Africans who face unemployment, a largely untransformed economic system and ongoing racism. Zuma's toyi-toyi song was an obvious echo of a time when the spectacular reigned supreme and, according to Ndebele, thereby kept "the larger issues of our society in our minds". Ndebele's own response to Zuma's spectacle was two-fold. He asked that Zuma think about the damage of his chosen performances of masculine bravado against the claimed internal ANC conspiracy. Ndebele wrote:

Zuma must now call off his supporters. His ability to do so will expose him to yet another test. What are the limits of his capacity for self-mastery? This latter attribute is vital for whoever aspires to high office. It will enable him to spare me, and others among the public, the pain and revulsion I felt when I saw him on my television screen, calling for umshini wami. Was he knowingly and defiantly inviting me to make horrible connections between the AK-47 and the invasive penis? The public moral issues are as graphic as this. [. . .] That is why, as he sang and danced with his supporters, images of South Africa's raped mothers, sisters, daughters (some, infants), nieces, aunts, and grandmothers, raced through my mind, torturing me. Are their pain and the broad sense of public morality of little consequence in the settling of 'family' scores?

When Zuma appropriates "umshini wam" for personal use, he reminds his onlookers that he is a struggle veteran and whoever opposes him is the enemy. Later, his supporters outside the court room and elsewhere would label all those critical of Zuma as "dogs" and "counter-revolutionaries".

When Young Communists leader, and ANCYL spokesperson, Zizi Kodwa, was quoted widely in the South African press as saying that Zuma supporters would punish "dogs" and send them back to their handlers, many of Zuma's detractors, among them Ndebele's name was associated with such "dogs" and their "handlers". Kodwa made no secret that "dogs" included those who publicly criticised Zuma's utterances during the trial, inside and outside the court room. Two particular pronouncements by Zuma had earned him the wrath of feminist commentators. Firstly, Zuma had insisted that he had taken a shower to avoid HIV/AIDS infection after sex with the HIV-positive complainant. Secondly, Zuma had declared that a "visibly aroused woman" had to be sexually satisfied lest she lay false rape charges.

This language and iconography borrow from the old struggle grammar of the spectacle and pretend that the lines between the issues at stake are clearly drawn. In the 1980s, apartheid (prime) ministers, soldiers, informers and police officers were routinely called dogs. So, arguably, when Kodwa referred to Zuma's critics as dogs, he invited associations with unjust attacks. In his statement (and utterances by other Zuma allies discussed below), the vice-president of the ANC, and later president of the same organisation, became the archetypal wronged struggle hero. In a series of moves, ranging from his own self-positioning and claiming of a popular song as his own to Kodwa's utterances and later pronouncements, all who critiqued him in any way became 'sell-outs', 'dogs' and 'counter-revolutionaries'.

Such critics, then, became responsible for all of Jacob Zuma's difficulties, and were in cahoots with the complainant, Khwezi, and those who had 'conspired' against Zuma from within the ruling party. In such instances, it was clear that "[c]ausality is a matter of making simple connections in order to produce the most startling and shocking results".

When Zuma took up his metaphorical machine gun, he was implying that Khwezi, the complainant in the rape case, and all those who believed her and/or questioned his own behaviour were 'agents of the apartheid state'. He did not need to say this explicitly, as his colleagues later did in response to COPE (a party formed in 2008 by ex-ANC leaders), Ndebele, and others. Zuma needed to invoke apartheid and thereby index the ready anger in many Black South Africans' minds and hearts at any echo of it. As Ndebele would have it in his definition of the spectacle, Zuma here "calls for emotion rather than conviction; [… and] establishes a vast sense of presence without offering intimate knowledge."

When we look at the very public life of Oscar Pistorius, we can see a different form of hypermasculinity and a violent masculinity on the rise. It is the intersection of embodied masculinities celebrated in athletics, all forms of racing and rugby. Reeva Steenkamp occupied centre stage as her boyfriend and killer, Oscar Pistorius, stood trial to prove his case – that he didn't kill her in moment of rage, but actually mistook her for 'an intruder', whom he presumably intended to kill. That this high-profile case's defence essentially relied on the assumed appropriateness of pumping bullets into an intruder – code for young Black criminal – is a glimpse into how war talk works. Therefore, even if Steenkamp was not the intended target, such excessive violence was not in itself a problem, according to the defence strategy. There are legitimate and illegitimate targets for such violence, and Paralympians' girlfriends are simply not the legitimate targets, it would seem. Of course, evidence that calls to question this very premise on which defence in Pistorius's trial hinged, emerged and spoke quite eloquently in Melinda Ferguson and Patricia Taylor's *Oscar: an accident waiting to happen*, reverberating well into the court of public opinion. The court of public opinion matters not only in cases where violent men are defended, as in MaMkhize, the woman who was Zuma's most visibilised supporter outside court during his rape trial and the Pistorians, but also in a much more sophisticated unmasking of violent masculinities/war talk than is possible in our country's criminal justice system which reveals itself to be consistently hostile to women survivors and victims of hypermasculinity.

Rather than being a sudden occurrence, the masculinist spectacle makes sense alongside other cultures of gendering politics in South Africa. This may explain why it is inhabited by men who otherwise embraced heroic, militant masculinities within the liberation movement and sports.

Zuma's metaphorical machine gun may be seen as the precursor to Julius Malema and Zwelinzima Vavi's declarations that they would kill for him. It also anticipates the pronouncement of Jason Mkhwane, a regional ANCYL leader, that any opposition party formed by former ANC members should be exterminated like cockroaches, a position he held even though his attention has been drawn to the similarities it bears with the sentiments that enabled the Rwanda genocide. Mkhwane's responses, quoted in Mataboge's article, are worth reproducing here, alongside statements by other leaders within the alliance, who spoke out in war talk:

> I'm not feeling bad about that statement. All these people in Cope are behaving like cockroaches and should be destroyed. [. . .] they

are behaving like cockroaches and cockroaches should be killed.
[. . .] We're not talking about killing human beings here, we're
talking about cockroaches. When you see a cockroach in your
house what do you do? You kill it. [. . .] I want you to understand
how we're going to kill them: we'll mobilise all our forces, all our
masses and ensure that the ANC wins next year's elections.

Elsewhere, Julius Malema is quoted by Letsoalo and Rossouw as
saying:

[w]e called on ANCYL structures to be on alert.
Counterrevolutionary forces are moving to destroy the revolution.
They will find us ready, not to speak to them, but to dismiss them.
Defenders of the revolution are on alert to defend the revolution.
[...] Now we say, come 2009, [Zuma] will become president [of
the country] and only death can stop us from ensuring that this
happens.

On his part Bheki Ntshalintshali told Tabane and Rossouw that:

[w]e cannot have a judicial system that acts in the manner in which
our courts have acted. [...] No amount of threat will intimidate
Cosatu from talking about the conduct of the judiciary. We are not
going to be told that judges are angels. They take decisions under
the influence of liquor.

And Gwede Mantashe was quoted in Letsoalo as saying:

[h]e is the president of the ANC. You hit the head, you kill the
snake. When there is an attack on him, it is a concerted attack on
the head of the ANC.

These are not quotations from activists engaged in a real war. They
are statements of men in power to silence dissent.

Hypermasculinities do not only feature in war talk through
military and extermination metaphors of snakes and cockroaches,

however. They also emerge in the brazen admission by a man the South African media seems perpetually fascinated by: Kenny Kunene, who is a wealthy businessman with a criminal past and a penchant for public declarations of his own misogyny. When asked by Pearl Thusi on a Metro fm show she co-hosts with Phat Joe whether he had sex with his students in his past life as a teacher, Kunene reportedly admitted to doing so with students younger than sixteen, the legal age of consent as per the Sexual Offences Act. He was unfazed when Thusi declared that he had admitted to statutory rape. But Kunene went much farther than this, tweeting variously that he was 'gang raped' by women and enjoyed it. There are numerous problems with Kunene's use of rape here in both instances, problems that Jenny Thorpe has illustrated well and at length in "Consent is key KK", including first, his:

> emphasis on collecting women as objects of his desire clearly indicates that his masculinity is founded on problematic ideas of sexuality where men consume women, and where male virility and sexual prowess at the expense of narratives on women's pleasure, and at the expense of women's health.

Second:

> violence against women remains a joke to most South Africans, and that there is little understanding of the connection of social messages that sanction this violence (eg invite men to use their penises as a weapon) to the violence itself. Threatening someone with gang rape incites violence. Acting as if this is no big deal promotes myths that rape is not a serious crime.

Third, "[d]escribing his own consensual sex fest as rape further illustrates his ignorance, and diminishes the experience of rape survivors", and finally, "Kenny Kunene has admitted to being a statutory rapist, and has threatened violence against another woman. Claims of statutory rape should be investigated by the SAPS."

The objectification and interchangeability (disposability) of women, and the light-hearted description of consensual group sex with women as rape are layers through which Kunene trivialises and mocks rape performed by himself routinely – by his own admission – and by other rapists. Kunene knows that there will be no consequences for such utterances, that he will continue to be celebrated as a fascinating man who has wild relationships with women. In public moments such as these, where rape is repeatedly mentioned as 'sex', fun and a joke, and when this can be done with no consequences, the hypocrisy of South African society, including the criminal justice system is laid bare. Many listeners to the national radio station, and readers of various newspapers reported this conversation, along with Kunene's own twitter timeline (which was also screen-grabbed and reposted) responding through further retreat into the 'rape joke' when several women and men challenged his war talk, his bravado, and alerted him to the consequences of his statements and tweets.

Kunene understands something that the rest of our society often pretends it does not know: that South Africa has a greater problem with the existence of the woman who speaks of having been raped, the young man with a broken body from rape, the old woman maimed and raped, and the child who needs reconstructive surgery than it does with the existence of a known, proud rapist. It is only the rape survivor and victim that trouble by pointing to her/his/their own pain in South African public culture. The rapist is welcome to live and boast and be celebrated or lambasted for his hypermasculinity, even as he continues to flourish financially.

In this regard, Kimberley Yates notes that spectacular masculinities, like "[a]ny system of domination ... dogmatically and inhumanely requires the immediate extermination of any views contrary to [their] own via severe punishment." Thus the complainant is accused of rape, and the rape survivor is mocked on a radio interview, newspapers and social media in a country where at the same time we do not understand why the rape statistics are so high, and why survivors are choosing not to turn to a criminal justice system that issues no consequences to public, recorded and witnessed admissions of rape.

The language used, collective memory evoked, bravado and masculinities referenced are those of defiance, resistance to oppression and ultimately triumph over apartheid for Zuma and his peers, and other adversity for Pistorius and Kunene; the effects of the masculinist spectacle in contemporary South Africa are violent. What needs emphasis and support, then, is, as Ndebele reminds us, "the sobering power of contemplation, of close analysis, and of the mature acceptance of failure, weakness and limitations."

Yet, in this contest, even if they will continue to be misrecognised as masculine weakness or even as unmanliness, positions against violent masculinities and war talk matter. It is important to continue to assert non-violent agency, responsibility and possibilities. In there lies the invitation to broaden public gender talk as well as our understanding of ourselves beyond limiting and violent performance. In his 1996 essay on Brenda Fassie, Njabulo Ndebele highlights the importance of a "politics of culture in creating a national identity", and argues that Brenda perfected a "complex network of communicating systems".

He insists that:

> her music, given the political context of a difficult struggle, helped to consolidate a view of culture as a site of social affirmation. Secondly, it contributed to a consolidation of a sense of South African musical space, familiar to millions across the land. Some symbols changed in the process. Stadiums associated with bogus independence became sites for a social assertiveness heavily suggested in Brenda's style.

One of the most powerful novels that seeks to make sense of rape histories, entanglements and the violent masculinities is Mtutuzeli Nyoka's beautiful *I speak to the silent*, a novel that stages this notion that part of what is required to undermine and undo rape culture and the violent masculinity spectrum is, as Mark Neal writes, to perform "publicly witnessed [instances where men] break ranks with patriarchy", where individual men "challenge the conventions of patriarchy, particularly when doing so in the name of black women" and such men also have to consciously police men's "own patriarchal priviledge". In this novel, refusal to be complicit is at the heart of masculinities that are open to transformation away from war talk to finding answers that heal and end rape culture. It is also important in Nyoka's vision that heroism be unmasked to reveal the mythologised violence at its core, as antidote to the current pervasive "masculine economy of representation, [where] the goal is to veil and hide oppression and its agents."

I have chosen not to represent and repeat Kunene's rape jokes in this chapter because I do not want to know how to repeat a rape joke. I realise that it would make reading this chapter easier. However, rape is not easy, and so I trust my readers to search for the 'rape jokes' themselves if they need to see them.

Conclusion

Writing this book has been a remarkable experience. I have felt compelled to write it, mainly because the bulk of the invitations to give public lectures over the past decades have been on rape specifically and gender-based violence more broadly. Since without exception, these invitations came from other feminist individuals and groups, I started thinking maybe all that material had to be collated and shaped into a book. I also imagined that this would be the easiest book I would ever write. Yet, many times I have told everybody in my life how I do not want to write it. I wish that I did not have to think about rape, that it was not so close to home, that I did not have to think about the many times I have felt the difficult combination of rage and tenderness as I sat across from someone as they talked about how someone had raped them. At the same time, rape occupies such a prominent place in many of the areas of research I am concerned with that I am certain to return to writing about rape in literary criticism. I wish it was possible to listen when a person speaks about being raped without feeling a rising sense of dread and nausea that someone would say something utterly vile in response. As if the trauma of rape is not enough, every day people in my country and the world use the fact of having survived rape to trivialise a survivor's value as a person, all the while pretending that they are 'just' trying to understand so the pain they inflict is out of place, due to oversensitivity, or in that cruel reversal, the accusation that the tale of rape silences those who have never experienced rape but continue to be complicit in a culture that enables rape. I look forward to being able to talk about rape without shaming rape survivors.

Pain is a valid source of knowledge, whether it be the pain of firsthand experience or empathetic pain. But empathy is not what most people feel when faced with a tale of rape told firsthand. Disbelief, questions, interrogation, demands for evidence and for behaviour to make the listener or reader feel better are the standard responses. Every woman and vulnerable man notices this done to those around them, constantly. It is a mystery and testament to the human spirit that rape survivors speak about it at all, outside of spaces designed for their healing.

The increase in the reporting of rape was much more likely the result of perceptions that the charges would be taken seriously than a result of increased occurrences of rape. In other words, post-1994, more and more women and other sexual minorities reported being raped to the police because a changing country, break the silence campaigns and a changing legal dispensation gave them confidence. Post-apartheid legislation has repeatedly been hailed for its pioneering pro-feminist stances. A significant part of the optimism that came with the release of Nelson Rolihlahla Mandela in February 1990 and the 27 April 1994 election was a shift in how we all thought about our lives as South Africans. The importance of telling our stories – whatever they may be – was central to nation-building efforts, crystallised in the Truth and Reconciliation Commission, but also finding echo in anti-rape and domestic abuse campaigns that reiterated the importance of breaking silence as a key to accessing freedom. This invitation to come to voice is not exclusively South African. It has long been a part of feminist consciousness raising where personal narratives of patriarchal wounding are shared in safe spaces. This sharing of personal narratives of patriarchal wounding is part of peeling away the layers of patriarchal violence.

However, while we all wished for a more open and more equitable sharing of narratives of human life, of what it means to have lived through apartheid, and what it means to be human in South Africa after the fall of the apartheid regime, the truth is that these stories were not unmediated by other ideas of who matters circulating in South Africa on both sides of the 27 April 1994 boundary. Not all stories matter in the same kind of way. Not all are allowed to see the light of day, immediately believed and valued. For, while speaking about trauma, difficulty and the previously silenced can offer enormous relief from a burden too long carried, empathy is not an automatic response. And even when it exists, it sometimes competes with other responses. The survivor often has to weigh up the impact of the possible responses. Under these conditions, then, not everything is utterable; many things remain unsayable.

When Beth Goldblatt and Sheila Meintjes first wrote, circulated and submitted their input to the TRC on the absence of women's testimonies, this is what they were alerting us to. As they noted, although many women appeared in front of the TRC, stories of women's lives under apartheid and of women's anti-apartheid activism were muted. Even as known women activists testified, they displaced their own experiences and activism. Goldblatt and Meintjes showed how, in the words of Barbara Boswell, "nationalist discourse has built the new South Africa upon the injustices visited upon the bodies of women." It was possible to talk about apartheid and its demise as though activism was made only through the energies of men. In this respect, we were hardly exceptional. Scholarship on nationalisms is unanimous in how masculinist national building narratives are. Goldblatt and Meintjes forced us to ask questions about how we might resist this process, why women were not speaking about their activism, and why their comrades were similarly silent. They also pointed to interviews and the archive of published activist women's autobiographies as a counter narrative. We had to ask, along with them, why some experiences remained unsayable, unspeakable even on a platform designed specifically to narrate that which had been silent. We also had to ask why sexual violence was equally silenced and expunged from men's testimonies, when, again, there was evidence of how rape and sexual torture of activist men was part of the apartheid state's manner of working.

Furthermore, although rape by agents of the apartheid state and in liberation movements remains muted, information about its presences and why it was unspeakable started to bubble to the surface. Out of nine thousand people who spoke at the TRC, only one, Rita Mazibuko spoke of her rape in the liberation movement. The responses to her testimony spoke volumes about why she was the only one even though as Goldblatt and Meintjes's report stated, many activist women confirmed rape in liberation movement sites. Responses to Mazibuko, as well as responses a decade later to another woman who accused a powerful hero of the struggle of rape, were clearly instructive.

It is in this context that Nthabiseng Motsemme insists that we need to read silences not as absences but as spaces rich with meaning. In asking why these silences exist, why they are forced and/or chosen, by whom and when, lies a wealth of knowledge.

Part of the apartheid archive is our failure to make any significant inroads into the scourge of violence against women. One of the ways we deal with it is through the recourse of 'breaking the silence' where until recently we understood this to mean that women should speak about their violation in order to turn the tide.

In Nyoka's novel *I speak to the silent* the author retains this unarticulated knowledge as a haunting that cannot be resolved through its denial, and as a haunting that threatens to render everything about the new nation a lie. Furthermore, through the title and how the silence is partially broken in the novel, Nyoka asks questions about complicity and the silent. The silent proliferate: they are Zodwa Mbete who witnesses the rapes and keeps quiet out of loyalty to her husband and the official narrative of her movement, the other comrades who do the same in the literary realm and beyond. Those who reject this silence of complicity even in the absence of real testimony at the TRC are those, like author Nyoka, who nonetheless force this consciousness on their readers – imagining fictional rapes in the place of those unclaimed and unrecognised, expanding that project that Zoë Wicomb inaugurated in her novel *David's Story* where she suggests the use of rape as one of the ways of making women cadres more compliant and enforcing discipline. Thus, to borrow from Helene Strauss's incisive analysis of Nyoka's novel:

> [g]uided by the silenced narrative of his daughter, Kondile's *call to the silent* can also be read as heeding *the call of the silenced*, who on the South African gender stage, feature primarily as women whose voices of trauma are muted by the epistemological constructions that safeguard ruling masculinities.

For Nyoka's and Wicomb's fictional projects, silence is fertile territory that can explain the contradictions of a new order and demonstrate continuities in how power works. Of course, Nyoka and Wicomb write fiction, but the point I am making here is that meanings created in fiction seep out into worlds beyond the fictional worlds of the novel. In other words, given the fact that many survivors would not come out directly to speak about their own sexual violation, even though some would feed into larger investigations as long as specific individuals were not identified, we have some idea of the tapestry of sexual violence under apartheid across political divides. This knowledge, even if it emerges as hints rather than clearly formulated narrative, needs to be woven into the narrative of South Africa's pasts, present and what we are still becoming. We cannot allow the silences to stand for absence, to say this never happened. This is where fiction helps. It allows us to flesh out the hints, suggestions and confirmed instances that are not fully told as stories. As Motsemme reminds us, "the mute always speak" – they speak when we allow recognition and imagination of what else happened in the past to co-exist.

For, while we do not readily speak of rape in our past, we know it forms an important part of the past. And this past further informs how we think about the present and future. This is not just true of the spaces that were explicitly concerned with defending or dismantling apartheid. It is also true of all of our everyday lives before, during and after apartheid.

I do not remember how old I was when I first became aware of rape as a thing in the world, as a possibility as well as something that happened to others with far-reaching effects. I recall knowing in primary school of the ways in which it was both fearful and not taken seriously. Rape was very confusing injustice, as girl students openly talked about how a certain girl expelled for falling pregnant had been impregnated by a certain teacher. As children we could not understand why she had to suffer, or why we were then subjected to many lessons about our morality and staying away from boys, when we could not imagine how a little girl could get away from a teacher. Teachers are powerful. I do not know how we knew for a fact about this girl, or several others, who all left school. I remember how certain girls and I talked obsessively among ourselves about what these girls had revealed. The expelled girls would talk to someone who would not keep the story to herself, sharing it with another girl thus creating this sense of 'everybody little' knowing.

I do not remember if we discussed it with boys, but we must have because many years later, some of my men school friends would share in this memory. I also remember the terror of those who felt sure that they were the next target of the specific teacher's inappropriate touching, cornering, making excuses to be in class alone with her. As an adult I know that this form of grooming is very common among paedophiles and other sex predators. We did not know the word rape, and we understood this man's behaviour as unfair and wrong as well as shameful because it was about sex in the end. We thought of this frightening sequence as linked to sex, which we also thought of as revolting and shameful.

Today, as an adult woman, I am devastated at the thought of the girls who never went back to school after their pregnancy, some of whom were beaten at home because they would not reveal who the boy was that had impregnated them. I remember how shamed they were for being pregnant as children, teenage mothers, and how slut-shamed they would sometimes be in later years. I wonder what it was that ensured that none of us told a parent, or any of the women teachers we loved and obsessed over, or the gentle man who taught us Afrikaans, made us feel safe, and who almost never caned anybody at a time when caning was as taken for granted a part of school life as chalk. We were tickled by his fear of caning us, as we understood it, and how even when he did cane, we would choose him over any of the other teachers. In retrospect, I think he just hated hitting children, avoided it and when he could not do so made sure it hurt as little as possible. Why didn't we tell our Science teacher, who was prone to bouts of strictness, but who also had the best sense of humour and made us love Science in a school that had no labs? Why not the principal, my father's friend, whose attempts at caning were so ridiculous as to be a constant preoccupation for little children? He had a thick log the length of a ruler to threaten us with, and I know firsthand that when he brought it down on your palm three times, it felt more like hand clapping than punishment, but we still feigned fear. He pretended he was interested in caning us, and we pretended to be afraid of the pain.

It does not matter how loved or taken care of by adults we felt, I know of no one who told an adult at school or at home. Yet, we could not understand how the adults either did not know or failed to do anything about it. Children sometimes imagine that adults are superhuman with psychic powers and unlimited eyes. It is fascinating to me that while we did not understand at all that the adults needed to be told in order to act to protect us from one of their own, we already had learnt too clearly the lesson about shame. In other words, even at primary school, where we did not know how to say 'rape', 'grooming', 'paedophile', or 'statutory rape', we understood shame as something that was never too far away.

In the columns written in 2013 by Ferial Haffajee that I discuss in an earlier chapter, she and her women friends would walk home from school very aware of their bodies, and fearful of what might happen to them. In this column, Haffajee links that fear and knowledge of their bodies as open to attack. She speaks of this fear as hers and her teenage women friends' constant shadow in public spaces, but also in the block where she lived. This is why she feels so protective of a school girl who tells her of her sexual harassment by a taxi driver on her way back from school shortly before writing the article. It is also how she tries to make sense of the continuities between her experience as a young woman, the school girl in the taxi and Anene Booysen. This vulnerability is not new, and although I disagree in identified ways with aspects of Haffajee's analysis of how Anene could have been safer from attack, what these columns reveal are the ways in which girls and young women feeling under siege is not a post-apartheid phenomenon. It makes sense for us to think of continuities rather than new phenomena. For Haffajee, there is an additional connection to the ways in which she secures her safety as an adult woman today.

When I was a student at the University of Cape Town in the early nineties, in the confusingly violent and hopeful days when apartheid was dying, I remember sitting on a residence interview committee constituted for some reprieve for the applicant the details of which I no longer remember. I was the House Government representative on this committee. At Tugwell House in those days, House Government meant the collective body for various student bodies in the residence, so it included student sub-wardens, corridor reps, head student receptionists, house committee, and so forth. Because the proceedings were to determine whether to let the applicants stay on in residence, or waive some fee, we were privy to some confidential information to assist us in making a decision. In several instances, the mitigating factor included a case of sexual assault.

I remember the absolute fear on the face of a woman I was well acquainted with through various overlapping networks who appeared in front of us, upon realising that I was part of the proceedings. She was not asked about her rape, but she spent considerable time explaining that she needed consideration for other factors that she attempted to de-link from the rape. It was clear to me then, as it is now, that she feared I might betray her confidence to her then partner, who was one of my closest friends. She knew that her boyfriend was growing increasingly frustrated with her changed behaviour, her distance, her emotional unavailability and her refusal to reveal what was wrong. He knew she was withholding something from him. She knew he and I confided in each other, and therefore felt unsafe with me knowing both that she had been raped and had tried to kill herself shortly after. It took many years of awkward conversation between us for her to realise that I would not tell him.

While I knew I could not tell him, I wondered for a long time about what kind of difference his knowledge would have made. Would he have understood and therefore figured out how to better support her, or would it have further complicated their relationship? As a lay Rape Crisis counsellor, I would be privy to a range of responses from loved ones who wanted to do the right thing, and what worked differed from person to person. The most important thing is that it was her story to tell, and writing about it now, with all identifying features expunged from the writing, is the first time I have spoken about it outside of that committee.

I have often thought of this story when faced with similar experiences in the last twenty years. Sometimes, when students and colleagues reveal abusive behaviour we may be able to interrupt if the survivor did not request that we hear the story in confidence, there can be a real quandary in identifying what the ethical responsibility is to the teller. So, even as we continue to work against sexual violence, and insist on distancing ourselves from complicities, we are keenly aware of the difficulties associated with the process.

Many people outside universities like to pretend to themselves that they imagine these spaces to be unaffected by the power dynamics that plague the rest of our society. Yet, as events that occasionally explode into the public domain reveal, this is far from true, whether we are speaking of sexual harassment by staff members caught or those still protected, the rape culture that some students are starting to write about in blogs that identify the writers as well as anonymous ones. The example of the woman who chose the pseudonym Lulu Diba, earlier in this book, is a particularly heartbreaking example of this.

Various feminists have argued that violence is one of the constitutive elements of South African society. It is such an intimate core that it grounds both historic and contemporary identity formation and contestation. In other words, explanations for the scourge of violence in South Africa need to be contextualised both against this backdrop of normalised and ingrained vast histories of violence and feminist understandings that misogynist and heteronormative violence are manifestations that reflect and perpetuate the very patriarchal nature of South African society.

Although feminists and other gender progressives would still wage critical war against gender-based violence under different circumstances, it is integral to the successes we carve to keep an eye on the myriad ways in which experiences and justifications of political violence are used to excuse and/or justify gender-based violence as well. South Africa is a country in deep denial about the causes of various phenomena such as gender-based violence.

As I put the last words down in this book, I realise how much the process of writing this has actually illuminated for me. One of the most frustrating things in my thinking and work on rape over the last two decades has been my inability to really understand how women who were themselves once raped do not feel empathy for those who speak of their own rape. I knew it had something to do with the way in which patriarchy says that women do not matter, that they/we are not fully human. In the language of Blackness, patriarchy really inculcates self-hate in women like all violent oppressive systems do. Yet, somehow this never felt like enough of an answer. I understood why survivors warn others against pressing charges or otherwise going public. What continued to bother me were the ways in which some survivors taunt and otherwise subject other survivors to secondary victimisation.

As I watch women question, taunt, disbelieve and help persecute other women who speak out against rape, the question has stayed with me. As I re-read an essay I was very familiar with, Yvette Abrahams's "Was Eva raped?" a different illumination came upon me, as I read the section on how rape makes the assaulted less than human. Abrahams writes that because rape changes a survivor's internal world in devastating ways, bringing about a real crisis in who she is and how things work, a survivor has to make sense of it somehow, and this is paramount. Therefore any meaning that allows her to make sense of it can be taken on board and used; even a meaning that engenders guilt in the survivor is preferable to helplessness. Preferable is not quite an appropriate word for what I mean here because this is a 'preference' in the absence of any healing, self-affirming resource. It is harder sometimes when faced with trauma to constantly revisit what she could have done differently than to arrive at a conclusion, even a harmful one. Abrahams writes:

> [h]umanness is a quality which is hard to live without. To react to rape by implicating oneself may not be the best reaction, but it is a workable one. Thus the dehumanisation of rape does not lie in the act alone, nor only in the memory of it, but in the trauma which induces the rape victim to deny her own subjectivity. Paradoxically, her path back to full humanness becomes blocked by the necessity of granting the rapist a human face.

We need to rethink how we move away from the current situation in which there is too little on holding perpetrators accountable. Although we have rendered gender-based violence abnormal in public talk and at legal level as successive feminists in the world, we have managed to do this without minimising it. It is still commonplace, and many violent men can just say they disapprove and distance themselves at the same time as going back to acting in violent ways.

It is imperative to create the kinds of realities that give survivors healthier choices to make sense of surviving rape, to look at the ways in which our tools have not only stopped working, but the many ways in which their co-option enables them to work in anti-feminist ways. I no longer think a small minority of men are holding us hostage. It is a painful realisation and way to live, and one that I have resisted for most of my life, and it may be one I will move through to discover joy on the other side.

In the meantime, I think we need to rebuild a mass-based feminist movement, a clearer sense of who our allies in this fight really are, to return to women's spaces as we develop new strategies and ways to speak again in our own name, to push back against the backlash that threatens to swallow us all whole. I also think we need to defend the terrain we are losing, because it seems to me that the backlash is working to keep more and more of us if not compliant, then afraid. Yet, a future free of rape and violence is one we deserve, and one we must create.

Bibliography

54 African women. 2006. "The Jacob Zuma case: a letter to Khwezi". Reprinted in Patrick Burnett, Shereen Karmali and Firoze Manji. Eds. *Grace, tenacity and eloquence: the struggle for women's rights in Africa*. Oxford & Nairobi: Fahamu, pp 162–166.

Abrahams, Yvette. 1996. "Was Eva raped? An exercise in speculative history". *Kronos* 23, pp 3–21.

Abrahams, Yvette. "The long great national insult". *Agenda* 32, pp 34–48.

Afrika, Nozizwe. 2006. "Letter to the Editor". *Mail and Guardian*, 17–23 March, p 24.

Alvi, Moniza. 2010. "Foreword: An Unsafe world". In Sorcha Gunne and Zoë Brigley Thompson. Eds. *Feminism, literature and rape narratives*. New York: Routledge, pp xi–xx.

Andrade, Susan. 2002. "Gender and the public sphere in Africa: writing women and rioting women". *Agenda* 54, pp 45–59.

Armstrong, Sue. 1994. "Rape in South Africa: an invisible part of apartheid's legacy". *Focus on Gender* 2.2, pp 3–39.

Atkins, Mike. 2006. "Letter to the Editor". *Mail and Guardian*, 19–25 May 2006, p 22.

Baderoon, Gabeba. 2014. "Hidden geographies of the Cape: shifting representations of slavery and sexuality in South African art and fiction". In Gwyn Campbell and Elizabeth Elbourne. Eds. *Sex, power and slavery*. Athens, OH: Ohio University Press, pp 417–432.

Baderoon, Gabeba. "Oblique Figures: Representations of Islam in South African Media and Culture". PhD Diss. University of Cape Town, 2004.

Baderoon, Gabeba. 2015. *Regarding Muslims: from slavery to post-apartheid*. Johannesburg: Wits University Press.

Baloyi, Robert. 2006. "Zuma's new role as Aids comedian". *City Press*, 16 April 2006, p 24.

Bam, A. 2006. "Letter to the Editor". *Mail and Guardian*, 19–25 May 2006, p 22.

Bates, Erin. 2015. "Fall of fame: Bob Hewitt's sentencing". *eNCA* http://www.enca.com/south-africa/fall-fame-bob-hewitts-sentencing. Accessed 10 June 2015.

Bathembu, Chris. 2008. "Malema being Probed by Police Over Outburst". *The Citizen*, 1 August 2008, p 4.

Bennett, Jane. 1997. "Credibility, plausibility and autobiographical oral narrative: some suggestions from the analysis of a rape survivor's testimony". In Ann Levett, Amanda Kottler, Erica Burman and Ian Parker. Eds. *Culture, power and difference: discourse analysis in South Africa*, pp 96–108.

Berger, Jonathan. 2006. "A is for arrogant, B is for brazen". *Mail and Guardian*, 31 March–6 April 2006, p 23.

Bhabha, Homi K. 2002. "A global measure". Inaugural lecture of the International and Interdisciplinary Graduiertenkolleg Postcolonial Studies of the Ludwig Maximilian University of Munich, Villa Stuck.

Biko, Steve. 1978. *I Write What I Like*. Ed. London: Borwedean.

Boswell, Barbara-Anne. 2010. "Black South African Women Writers: Narrating the Self, Narrating the Nation". PhD Diss. University of Maryland.

"Boy raped in initiation horror". *eNCA*, 6 February 2015.

Boya, Siya. 2015. "EC mum and farmer to plead guilty to child prostitution". *Daily Dispatch*, 7 May 2015. Accessed 11 June 2012, p 1.

Boya, Siya. 2015. "Judge hits out at child abuser". *Daily Dispatch*, 8 May 2015. http://www.dispatchlive.co.za/news/judge-hits-out-at-child-abuser. Accessed 11 June 2012.

Boya, Siya. 2015. "Woman alleged to have 'offered' girls to farmer for compensation". *Daily Dispatch*, 6 May 2015. http://www.dispatchlive.co.za/news/woman-alleged-to-have-offered-girls-to-farmer-for-compensation. Accessed 11 June 2012.

Campbell, Gwyn and Elizabeth Melbourne. Eds. 2014. *Sex, power and slavery*. Athens, OH: Ohio University Press.

Cele, Zanele. 2006. "Zuma's behaviour appalling". *City Press*, 26 March 2006, p 24.

City Press reporter. "Rape is a vicious form of violence against women". *City Press*, 12 March 2006, p 1.

Cock, Jacklyn. 1991. *Colonels and Cadres: War and Gender in South Africa*. Cape Town: Oxford University Press.

Cock, Jacklyn. 1993. "The place of women in the demilitarisation agenda". *Agenda* 16, pp 49–55.

Coetzee, Frans. 2002. "Potse denies rape of Tshepang". *News24*, 25 July 2002. http://www.news24.com/xArchive/Archive/Potse-denies-rape-of-Tshepang-20020625. Accessed 29 January 2015.

Cole, Johnetta Betsch, and Guy-Sheftall, Beverly. 2003. *Gender Talk: The Struggle for Women's Equality in African-American Communities*. New York: One World.

Cravens, Mary Caroline. 2009. "Manumission and the Life Cycle of a Contained Population: The VOC Lodge Slaves at the Cape of Good Hope, 1680–1730". In Rosemary Brana-Shute and Randy J Sparks. Eds. *Paths to Freedom: Manumission in the Atlantic World*. Columbia: University of South Carolina Press, pp 97–120.

Dabydeen, David. 1984. "Preface". *Slave song*. London: Peepal Tree Press.

Davis, David Brion. 2014. "Slavery, sex and dehumanization". In Gwyn Campbell and Elizabeth Elbourne. Eds. *Sex, power and slavery*. Athens, OH: Ohio University Press, pp 15–31.

Desai, Rehad. Dir. 2014. *Miners shot down*. Johannesburg: Uhuru Productions.

Dibetle, Monako. 2006. "JZ still the workers' darling?" *Mail and Guardian*, 31 March–6 April 2006, p 6.

Dikeni, Sandile. 2011. "Charterists: youth identity in the 80s". *Umrabulo*. 11, 2nd quarter. http://www.anc.org.za/show.php?id=2945. Accessed 10 February 2015.

Direko, Redi. 2006. "Jacob Zuma is the weakest link in a proud Zulu culture". *City Press*, 9 April 2006, p 21.

Edgerton, Robert E. 2009. *Africa's armies from honor to infamy: a history from 1791 to the present*. New York: Basic Books.

Emerson, Rana A. 2002. "'Where my girls at': Negotiating Black Womanhood in Music Videos". *Gender and Society* 16, pp 115–135.

Gasa, Nomboniso. 2007a. "Feminisms, motherisms, patriarchies and women's voices in the 1950s". In *Basus' iimbokodo, bawel' imilambo/ They remove boulders and cross rivers: Women in South African History*. Ed. Nomboniso Gasa. Cape Town: HSRC Press, pp 207–229.

Gasa, Nomboniso. 2007b. "Let them build more gaols". In *Basus' iimbokodo, bawel' imilambo/They remove boulders and cross rivers: Women in South African History*. Ed. Nomboniso Gasa. Cape Town: HSRC Press, pp 129–152.

Gasa, Nomboniso. 2007c. "Feminisms, Motherisms, Patriarchies and Women's Voices in the 1950s". In *Basus' Iimbokodo, Bawel' Imilambo/They Remove Boulders and Cross Rivers: Women in South African History*. Ed. Nomboniso Gasa. Cape Town: HSRC Press, pp 207–29.

———. 2006. "Dear Jacob, I feel pain …". *Mail and Guardian*, 17–23 March 2006, p 23.

Gauntlett, David. 2003. *Media, gender and identity: an introduction*. New York and London: Routledge.

Gcwensa, Lindani. 2006. "Letter to the Editor". *Mail and Guardian*, 19–25 May 2006, p 22.

Germaner, Shain. 2015. "Hewitt sentenced to six years in jail". *The Star*, 18 May 2015.

Gerntholtz, Liezl. 2006. "Comment: The law can work for women". *Mail and Guardian*, March 31–6 April 2006, p 6.

Gordimer, Nadine. 1998. *The House Gun*. Cape Town: David Philip.

Govender, Prega. 2015. "Mop handle rapists should be expelled". *Sunday Times*, 8 February 2015. http://www.timeslive.co.za/local/2015/02/08/mop-handle-rapists-should-be-expelled-1. Accessed 20 May 2015.

Govender, Pregs. 2006. "Strike a woman, strike a rock". *Mail and Guardian* ,17–23 March 2006, p 5.

Gqola, Pumla Dineo. 2006a. "Bleeding on the streets of South Africa". *Mail and Guardian*, 12–18 May 2006, p 29.

———. 2006b. "The hype of women's empowerment". *Mail and Guardian*, 23–30 November 2006. http://mg.co.za/article/2006-11-27-the-hype-of-womens-empowerment. Accessed 20 July 2015.

———. 2006c. "Gender talk is seriously flawed". *Cape Times*, 27 November 2006.

Gqola, Pumla Dineo. 2001a. "Contradictory locations: Blackwomen and the Black Consciousness Movement (BCM) in South Africa". *Meridians: Feminism, Race, Transnationalism* 2. 2, pp 130–152.

Gqola, Pumla Dineo. 2001b. "Defining people: analysing power, language and the metaphors of the new South Africa". *Transformation: Critical*

Perspectives on Southern Africa 47, pp 94–106.

Gqola, Pumla Dineo. 2013. *A Renegade called Simphiwe*. Auckland Park: Melinda Ferguson/Jacana Media.

Gqola, Pumla Dineo. 2015. *What is slavery to me? postcolonial/ slave memory in post-apartheid South Africa*. Johannesburg: Wits University Press.

———. 2009. "'The difficult task of normalising freedom': spectacular masculinities, Ndebele's literary/cultural commentary and post-apartheid life". *English in Africa*, 36.1 pp 61–76.

Gqola, Pumla Dineo. 2007a. "How the 'Cult of Femininity' and Violent Masculinities Support Endemic Gender Based Violence in South Africa". *African Identities* 5.1, pp 111–24.

———. 2007b. "'Like Three Tongues in One Mouth': Tracing the Elusive Lives of Slave Women in (Slavocratic) South Africa". *Basus' Iimbokodo, Bawel' Imilambo/They Remove Boulders and Cross Rivers: Women in South African History*. Ed. Nomboniso Gasa. Cape Town: HSRC Press, pp 21–41.

———. 2004. "Shackled Memories and Elusive Discourses? Colonial Slavery and the Contemporary Cultural and Artistic Imagination in South Africa". PhD Diss. University of Munich.

Grant, Kevin. Ed. 1997. *The Art of David Dabydeen*. London: Peepal Tree Press.

Gunne, Sorcha and Zoe Brigley Thompson. 2010. Eds. *Feminism, literature and rape narratives – violence and violation*. London: Routledge.

Gxwazi, Mpendulo. 2006. "Zuma cannot be trusted". *City Press*, 9 April 2006, p 24.

Haffajee, Ferial. 2013. "#WTF was she thinking?" *City Press*, 11 February 2013. http://www.news24.com/Columnists/Ferial-Haffajee/ WTF-was-she-thinking-20130211. Accessed 29 March 2014.

———. "Editor's note: Words fail us". *City Press*, 10 February 2013. http://www.news24.com/Archives/City-Press/Editors-note-Words-fail-us-20150429. Accessed 29 March 2014.

Hansson, Desireé. 1993. "A shock to the system". *Agenda* 16, pp 10–18.

Hassim, Shireen. 2005a. "Terms of engagement: South African challenges". *Feminist Africa* 4, pp 29–45.

Hassim, Shireen. 2006. *Women's Organisations and Democracy in South Africa: Contesting Authority*. Madison, WI: Wisconsin University Press.

Hassim, Shireen. 2009a. "After apartheid: consensus, contention, and gender in South Africa's public sphere". *International Journal of Politics, Culture and Society* 22.4, pp 453–464.

Hassim, Shireen. 2009b. "Democracy's shadows: sexual rights and gender politics in the rape trial of Jacob Zuma". *African Studies* 68.1, pp 57–77.

Hlongwa, Wonder and S'thembiso Msomi. "'Unsafe': JZ Accuser Relocated". *City Press*, 16 April 2006, p 2.

hooks, bell. 1989. *Talking Back: Thinking Feminist,Thinking Black*. Boston, MA: South End Press.

Irish, Jenni. 1993. "Massacres, muti and misery". *Agenda* 16, pp 6–9.

Klein, Amelia Ann. 2010. "The demographic profile and psychosocial history of a group of convicted perpetrators of the rape of children under three years". PhD Diss. University of the Witwatersrand.

Knoetze, Daneel. 2015. "Child rape case – how poor families struggle for justice". *Groundup*. http://groundup.org.za/article/child-rape-case-how-poor-families-struggle-justice_2712. Accessed 11 June 2015.

Kobe, Mkhululi. 2006. "JZ fails moral judgement test". *City Press*, 16 April 2006, p 24.

Kruger, Hendrika. 2006. "Jacob Zuma is guilty of immoral behaviour". *City Press*, 9 April 2006, p 24.

Lebelo, Luther. 2006. "Letter to the Editor". *Mail and Guardian*, 19–25 May 2006, p 22.

Letsoalo, Matuma, Mandy Rossouw and Sello S Alcock. "Mantashe Attacks!" *Mail and Guardian*, 4–10 July 2008, p 2.

——— and Mandy Rossouw. "Tensions simmer in Rebel Camp". *Mail and Guardian*, 10–18 Oct 2008, p 2.

Lewis, Desiree. 1992. "Myths of motherhood and power: the construction of 'Black women' in literature". *English in Africa* 19.1, pp 35–51.

Loomba, Ania. 1998. *Colonialism/Postcolonialism*. New York: Routledge.

Lorde, Audre. 1984. *Sister Outsider: Essays and Speeches*. New York: Crossing Press Feminist Series.

Ludwig, Vanessa. 2006. "Justice with dignity". *Pambazuka*: weekly forum for social justice in Africa. 11 May, archived at http://www.pambazuka.org/en/category/comment/34139. Reprinted in Patrick Burnett, Shereen Karmali and Firoze Manji. Eds. *Grace, tenacity and eloquence: the struggle for women's rights in Africa*. Oxford & Nairobi: Fahamu, pp 17–176.

Magagula, Sipho. 2006. "Letter to the Editor". *Mail and Guardian*, 17–23 March 2006, p 24.

Magubane, Zine. *Bringing the empire home: race, class and gender in Britain and colonial South Africa*. Chicago: Chicago University Press.

Mail and Guardian editorial. 2014. "Deep flaws on display". 17–23 March, p 24.

———. 2006. "Phansi com-tsotsis!" 10–16 March 2006, p 22.

Majavu, Anna. 2012. "How a rape judgement fails vulnerable children all over South Africa". *South African Civil Society Information Service*. http://sacsis.org.za/site/article/1502. Accessed 26 November 2012.

Makhanya, Mondli. 2006. "Zuma needs to stop himself being seen as a latter-day Buthelezi". *Sunday Times*, 9 April 2006, p 20.

Mataboge, Mmanaledi. "The ANCYL's 'Cockroach' Fumigator". *Mail and Guardian*, 28 November–4 December 2008, p 2.

Matsobe, Mashego. 2006. "Zuma went against what he preached". *City Press*, 16 April 2006, p 24.

Mayne, Anne. 1993. "Discourse on damage". *Agenda* 16, pp 19–32.

Mbembe, Achille. 2001. *On the Postcolony*. Berkeley, CA: University of California Press.

Medical Research Council and Gender Links. 2011. "The War at home: gender based violence indicators project – Gauteng Research Report.". http://www.genderlinks.org.za/article/the-war-at-home---gbv-indicators-project-2011-08-16. Accessed 12 December 2011.

Mkhize, Nonhlanhla. 2006. "Letter to the Editor". *Mail and Guardian*, 17–23 March 2006, p 24.

Mnisi, Phillimon. 2006. "Letter to the Editor". *Mail and Guardian*, 17–23 March 2006, p 24.

Moffett, Helen. 2006. "'These women, they force us to rape them': rape as narrative of social control in post-apartheid South Africa". *Journal of Southern African Studies* 32.1, pp 129–144.

Mogotsi, Lesego Sechaba. 2006. "Letter to the Editor". *Mail and Guardian*, 17–23 March 2006, p 24.

Mohomane, Nonkululeko. 2006. "Letter to the Editor". *Mail and Guardian*, 17–23 March 2006, p 24.

Mokoena, Ben. 2006. "Media seem hellbent on destroying Zuma". *Sunday Times*, 16 April 2006, p 18.

Molele, Charles, Moipone Malefane and Ndivhuho Mafela. 2006. "The world according to Jacob Zuma". *Sunday Times*, 9 April 2006, p 13.

————. 2006. "Supporters lambaste 'impertinent' prosecutor". *Sunday Times*, 9 April 2006, p 13.

Molope, Kagiso Lesego. 2012. *This Book Betrays My Brother*. Cape Town: Oxford University Press.

Moodley, Asha. 1993. "Black woman you are on your own". *Agenda* 16, pp 44–48.

Morata, Ntwampe. 2006. "Letter to the Editor". *Mail and Guardian*, 17–23 March 2006, p 24.

Motsemme, Nthabiseng. 2002. "Y-Freedom: Nthabiseng Motsemme on Blackness in postapartheid South Africa". *Wiser in Brief*, November 2002, pp 14–15.

Motsemme, Nthabiseng. 2004. "The mute always speak: on women's silences at the Truth and Reconciliation Commission". *Current Sociology* 52. 5, pp 909–932.

Moya, Fikile-Ntsikelelo. 2006. "She isn't my daughter". *Mail and Guardian*, 31 March–6 April 2006, p 6.

Moya, Fikile-Ntsikelelo. 2006. "In defence of Kemp J Kemp". *Mail and Guardian*, 31 March– 6 April 2006, p 23.

Mpempe, Jabu. 2006. "Direko's stance on trial is partial". *City Press*, 16 April 2006, p 24.

Msomi, S'thembiso. 2006. "Can JZ bail himself out?" *City Press*, 2 April 2006, p 1.

Msomi, S'thembiso. 2006. "Day of reckoning in the dock for Msholozi". *City Press*, 2 April 2006, p 23.

Msomi, S'thembiso. 2006. "Sika lekhekhe, sika lekhekhe!" *City Press*, 16 April 2006, p 21.

Mukhuthu, Zwanga. 2014. "Dad in dock for child rape". *Daily Dispatch*, 18 February 2014. http://www.dispatchlive.co.za/news/dad-in-dock-for-child-rape. Accessed 20 May 2015.

Musekwa, Philip. 2006. "Letter to the Editor". *Mail and Guardian*, 17–23 March 2006, p 24.

Musila, Grace. 2009. "Phallocracies and gynocratic transgressions: gender, state power and Kenyan public life". *Africa Insight* 39.1, pp 39–57.

Musila, Grace. 2014. "The idiot's guide to misogyny: East and South African edition". *Voices of Africa*. http://voicesofafrica.co.za/idiots-guide-misogyny-east-south-african-edition. Accessed 15 February 2015.

Myers, Alex. 2006. "Letter to the Editor". *Mail and Guardian*, 19–25 May 2006, p 22.

Nair, Roshila. 2001. "Aluta continua". *Agenda: Empowering Women for Gender Equity* 50, p 128.

Naylor, Nikki. 2006. "The socio-political eunuch called an impartial judge". *Pambazuka*: weekly forum for social justice in Africa. 11 May, archived at http://www.pambazuka.org/en/category/comment/34140. Reprinted in Patrick Burnett, Shereen Karmali and Firoze Manji. Eds. *Grace, tenacity and eloquence: the struggle for women's rights in Africa*. Oxford & Nairobi: Fahamu, pp 177–180.

Ndashe, Sibongile. 2006. "Can I speak, please?" *Pamabazuka*: weekly forum for social justice in Africa. 11 May, archived at http://www.pambazuka.org/en/category/comment/34138. Reprinted in Patrick Burnett, Shereen Karmali and Firoze Manji. Eds. *Grace, tenacity and eloquence: the struggle for women's rights in Africa*. Oxford & Nairobi: Fahamu, pp 171–173.

Ndebele, Njabulo S. 1991. *Rediscovery of the Ordinary*. Johannesburg: COSAW.

———. 2007. *Fine Lines from the Box: Further Thoughts about Our Country*. Houghton: Umuzi.

———. 1998. "Memory, Metaphor, and the Triumph of Narrative". *Negotiating the Past: The Making of Memory in South Africa*. Ed. Sarah Nuttall and Carli Coetzee. Cape Town: Oxford University Press, pp 19–28.

Neal, Mark Anthony. 2005. *New Black Man*. New York: Routledge.

Ngobese, Castro. "YCL Statement on Media Briefing by Terror Lekota". *Mail and Guardian*, 17–23 October 2008, p 26.

Ngqu. 2006. "Letter to the Editor". *Mail and Guardian*, 19–25 May 2006, p 22.

Ngqumetyana, Mbulelo. 2006. "Direko's views on Mosholozi spot-on". *City Press*, 16 April 2006, p 24.

Nichols, Grace. 1983. *I Is a Long Memoried Woman*. London: Karnak.

Nkutha, Lindiwe. "Dear Diary". In Pamabazuka: weekly forum for social justice in Africa. 11 May, archived at http://www.pambazuka.org/en/category/comment/34141. Reprinted in Patrick Burnett, Shereen Karmali and Firoze Manji. Eds. *Grace, tenacity and eloquence: the struggle for women's rights in Africa*. Oxford & Nairobi: Fahamu, pp 181–184.

Ntantala, Phylis. 2008. "Black women intellectuals and the struggle for liberation." Public Lecture presented for the Platform for Public Deliberation, University of the Witwatersrand, 8 August 2008.

Nyoka, Mtutuzeli. 2004. *I Speak to the Silent*. Scottsville: KwaZulu-Natal University Press.

O fm. "Bob Hewitt removed from Hall of Fame after sex scandal". 16 November 2012. http://www.ofm.co.za/article/National/125923/Bob-Hewitt-removed-from-tennis-Hall-of-Fame-after-sex-scandal. Accessed 20 May 2015.

Palmer, Robin. 2006. "Sex, lies and agendas". *Sunday Times*, 14 May 2006, p 39.

Peterson, Bhekizizwe. 2012. "Dignity, memory and truth under siege: reconciliation and nation building in post-apartheid South Africa". In Sam Okoth Opondo and Michael J Shapiro. Eds. *The New Violent Cartography: geo-analysis after the aesthetic turn*. London: Routledge, pp 214–233.

Pillay, Deneesha. 2015. "Farmer who paid domestic to prostitute her daughter gets 15 years". *The Herald*, 8 May 2015. http://www.heraldlive.co.za/farmer-paid-domestic-prostitute-daughter-gets-15-years. Accessed 10 May 2015.

Pillay, Deneesha. 2015. "Nine sex slave probes in the Eastern Cape". *The Herald* ,12 May 2015.

Pillay, Deneesha. 2015. "Pair to plead guilty to child prostitution". *The Herald*, 7 May. http://www.heraldlive.co.za/pair-plead-guilty-child-prostitution. Accessed 9 May 2015.

Pillay, Navi. 1993. "Judges and gender". *Agenda* 9, pp 47–50.

Pityana, Barney. 2006. "The Zuma saga spells the very abyss of moral degeneration". *Mail and Guardian*, 10–16 March 2006, p 25.

Pringle, Thomas. 1831. "Preface". In Mary Prince. *The History of Mary Prince: a West Indian Slave Related by Herself*. London.

Quinn, Beth A. 2002. "Sexual harassment and masculinity: the power and meaning of 'girl watching'". *Gender and Society* 16, pp 386–402.

Ramjettan, Trivern. 2006. "Letter to the Editor". *Mail and Guardian*, 19–25 May 2006, p 22.

Ramphele, Mamphela. 1996. "Political widowhood in South Africa: the embodiment of Ambiguity". *Daedelus: Journal of the American Academy of Arts and Sciences* 125.1, pp 9–118.

Rawoot, Ilham. 2011. "Mogoeng's shocking child rape rulings". *Mail and*

Guardian. http://mg.co.za/article/2011-09-02-mogoengs-shocking-child-rape-rulings. Accessed 11 June 2015.

Rizos, Dominique. 2010. "Lad Magazines, Raunch Culture and the Pornification of South African media". MA Diss. University of the Witwatersrand.

———. 2012. "Lad Magazines, Raunch Culture and the Increasing Pornification of South African Media". *Agenda* 26.3, pp 38–49.

Ronyuza, Mzukisi. 2006. "Letter to the Editor". *Mail and Guardian,* 19–25 May 2006, p 22.

Rossouw, Mandy. "Rolling Action for Zuma". *Mail and Guardian,* 26–31 July 2008, p 8.

Russell, Diana. 1993. "The story of Lulu Diba". *Agenda* 16, pp 6–80.

Salo, Elaine. 2005a. "Gender based violence and sexuality in South Africa". Harold Wolpe Memorial Trust Open Dialogue Event, 23 March 2005.

Salo, Elaine. 2005b. "Multiple targets, mixing strategies: complicating feminist analysis of contemporary South African women's movements". *Feminist Africa* 4, pp 64–71.

Samuelson, Meg. 2009. "Walking through the door and inhabiting the house: South African literary culture and criticism after the transition". *English Studies in Africa* 52.1, pp 130–137.

SAPS Journal. 2014. "Eastern Cape duo in court for sexually exploiting three girls". 13 August 2014.

Scully, Pamella. 1997. *Liberating the family? Gender and British slave emancipation in the rural Western Cape, South Africa, 1823–1853.* Portsmouth, NH: Heinemann.

Sefara, Makhudu. 2006. "Zuma's harrowing week of shockers in the dock". *City Press,* 9 April 2006, p 21.

Segalwe, Oupa. 2014. "Public Protector Thuli Madonsela on change of strategy in fight against women and child abuse". 26 November 2014. http://www.gov.za/subject-public-protector-calls-approach-change-fight-against-women-child-abuse. Accessed 20 December 2014.

Sephuma, Thabo oa. 2006. "Zuma is failing fight on Aids". *City Press,* 26 March 2006, p 24.

Sesotlho, Mongezi. 2006. "Rape is rape no matter the circumstances". *City Press,* 9 April 2006, p 24.

Shire, Warsan. 2011. *Teaching Mother how to give birth.* London: Mouthmark.

Smith, Gail. 2006. "Survivors of sexual violence lift the lid on their ordeals". *City Press*, 19 March 2006, p 27.

———. 2006. "Zuma judge erred in denying women's groups". *City Press*, 9 April 2006, p 22.

Stegeman, Kate. "Remembering Anene Booysen: The sound, the fury and the politicking". *Mail and Guardian*. 11 February 2013. http://mg.co.za/article/2013-02-11-remembering-anene-booysen-the-sound-the-fury-and-the-politicking. Accessed 20 May 2014.

Strauss, Helene. 2009. "Memory, masculinity and responsibility: Searching for 'good men' in Mtutuzeli Nyoka's *I speak to the silent*". *English in Africa* 36.1, pp 77–89.

Suttner, Raymond. 2009. "The Jacob Zuma rape trial: power and African National Congress (ANC) masculinities". *Nora* 17.3, p 222–236.

Tabane, Rapule and Mandy Rossouw. 2008. "Attacks on the Judiciary". *Mail and Guardian*, 8–14 August 2008, p 2.

———. 2008. "Scramble to Secure a Zuma Presidency". *Mail and Guardian*, 8–14 August 2008, p 2.

Thamm, Marianne. 2002. *Mental Floss: A Collection of 'Unfair Comment' from Fairlady*, Spearhead, Claremont.

Thompson, Zoë Brigley and Sorcha Gunne. 2010. "Introduction: Feminism without borders: The Potentials and Pitfalls of Retheorizing Rape". In Sorcha Gunne and Zoë Brigley Thompson. Eds. *Feminism, literature and rape narratives*. New York: Routledge, pp 1–22.

Thorpe, Jenny. 2013. "Consent is key, KK". *Thoughtleader*, 15 April 2013. http://www.thoughtleader.co.za/jenniferthorpe/2013/04/15/consent-is-king-kk. Accessed 29 January 2015.

Tjempe, Tshepiso. 2006. "Can Direko expect to be taken seriously?" *City Press*, 16 April 2006, p 24.

Tlali, Miriam. 1989. *Footprints in the Quag*. Claremont: David Philip.

Tsedu, Mathatha. 2006. "Callous do-gooders had no care for Zuma's accuser". *City Press*, 2 April 2006, p 23.

Vetten, Lisa. 2007. "Violence against women in South Africa". In Sakhela Buhlungu, John Daniel, Roger Southall and Jessica Lutchman. Eds. *State of the nation: South Africa 2007*. Cape Town: HSRC Press, pp 425–442.

Vetten, Lisa and Liezl Gernholtz. 2006. "Zuma trial: lessons for future rape trials". *South African Labour Bulletin* 30.3, p 55.

Werth, Carl. 2006. "Letter to the Editor". *Mail and Guardian*, 19–25 May 2006, p 22.

Wicomb, Zoë. 2000. *David's Story*. Cape Town: Kwela.

"Women – a call to action". Statement released by delegates to the Women Leading the Way: health, wealth and peace conference, Gordon Institute of Business Science, 8–10 March 2006.

Yates, Kimberley A. 1997. "The madness of the Black man on his own: An analysis of the silences of history, in search of herstory". MA Diss. University of Cape Town.

Yates, Kimberley A. and Gqola, Pumla Dineo. 1998. "'Some kind of madness': Mamphela Ramphele on being Black, female and transgressive". *Agenda* 37, pp 90–95.

Zuzile, Mphumzi. 2013. "Elderly deaf woman raped and mutilated". *Daily Dispatch,* 5 December 2013. http://www.dispatchlive.co.za/news/elderly-deaf-woman-raped-and-mutilated. Accessed 20 March 2015.

PRAISE FOR *A RENEGADE CALLED SIMPHIWE*

*"The clarity of Gqola's writing is astounding, her thinking
sturdy and easy to follow as a bridge through the spaces
she describes Dana moving to and from."*

– GENNA GARDINI, CAPE TIMES

"Something totally different ... intellectually stimulating."

– BLAQUE MAGAZINE

*"A credit on the book's front cover by Professor Njabulo
Ndebele reads, 'Pumla Gqola's mind exhilarates ... Here's
a literary presence that makes thinking a pleasure.' I
couldn't agree more."*

– ZANELE SABELA, DESTINY MAN

*"This book will go down as a cornerstone in South African
feminist works on a public figure ... The greatest strength
of this book is Gqola's relentless attention to an African
feminist aesthetic."*

– HUGO CANHAM, BooksLIVE

*"Despite it being written by someone in academia,
it is fortunately for the reader as painless and enjoyable
as it is profound."*

– ZUKISWA WANNER, JAMES MURUA'S LITERATURE BLOG

*"Gqola presents you with a one of a kind of book, one she
describes as 'the kind of book I would like to read'. While
the book does explore a variety of things, it's quite clearly
written with an intensive view on the relations of males and
females in the patriarchal society. It opens you up to
a large number of truths."*

– TSHEPO JAMILLAH MOYO, THE TSWANA TIMES

"*Gqola has an intense appreciation for textual aesthetics.*"

– ELELWANI RAMUGONDO, *JENDA JOURNAL*

"*Doors of insight open up a page with daring freshness.
Here is a literary presence that makes thinking a pleasure.*"

– NJABULO S NDEBELE, WRITER AND ACADEMIC

"*I enjoyed* A Renegade Called Simphiwe *immensely.
Gqola's conversational style of 'thinking about Simphiwe
out loud' is accessible and stimulating. The author is an
acclaimed literary scholar and feminist, and this recent
publication shows her strength as a non-fiction writer.
A Renegade Called Simphiwe explores the presence of
Simphiwe Dana in the various public arenas she occupies;
as SAMA award-winning musician, as Twitter activist, as
'soft-feminist' and as renegade.*"

– MARIA GEUSSTYN, STELLENBOSCH LITERARY PROJECT

"*The book wonderfully mimics the contradictions that
its subject embodies, blending the passionate play of
emotional involvement with the rigour of academia to
produce a book that is both a pleasure to read and a
spur to introspection.*"

– CHRIS ROPER, MAIL & GUARDIAN

"*Her writing is intriguing, fun and relatable. Her
new book* A Renegade Called Simphiwe *has those
characteristics. I enjoyed reading the book from the
first chapter until the last.*"

– LEBOGANG MGIBA, BLAQUE MAGAZINE